UP YOUR ATTITUDE!

Changing the Way You Look At Life

by
Elwood N. Chapman

CRISP PUBLICATIONS, INC.
Menlo Park, California

18.95

UP YOUR ATTITUDE!
Changing the Way
You Look At Life

Elwood N. Chapman

CREDITS
Editor: **Michael Crisp**
Layout and Composition: **Interface Studio**
Cover Design: **Sam Concialdi**
Artwork: **Interface Studio**

Copyright © 1993 by Crisp Publications, Inc.
Printed in the United States of America

Library of Congress Cataloging-in-Publication Data
Chapman, Elwood N.
  Up your attitude! : changing the way you look at life / by Elwood
N. Chapman.
     p. cm.
  ISBN 1-56052-234-8 :
  1. Attitude (Psychology)   2. Attitude change.   3. Happiness.
I. Title.   93-13315
158--dc20   CIP

This book is printed on recyclable paper with soy ink.

Reader's/Reviewers Comments

"Elwood Chapman has helped millions of people understand and improve their attitudes. He really is Mr. Attitude."

Richard Knowdell
President, Career Research & Testing

"What can I say! Elwood Chapman is the Thomas Edison of attitude. If he didn't invent it, he perfected it. *UP YOUR ATTITUDE* should be read by everyone."

Robert Maddux
Vice President, Right Associates

"On my last business trip, I encountered at least a dozen people who needed this friendly book. Pass your copy around. A lot of people need the message it delivers!"

Louise Berman
Retirement Planner

"I expect to make this required reading of all of my hospitality students. Nothing is more important than your attitude!"

William Martin, Ph.D.
Professor of Hospitality Management

"All of us encounter down times. *UP YOUR ATTITUDE* is great for turning things around. I'm refreshed every time I pick it up."

Paul Timm
Author of *RECHARGE YOUR CAREER & YOUR LIFE*

"There simply is no one better qualified to write a book on attitude than Elwood Chapman."

Cynthia Scott
Author of *TAKE THIS JOB AND LOVE IT*

Other Books by the Author

Elwood Chapman has authored more than 25 books that have aggregrate sales in the millions. A few of his best known titles are listed below:

YOUR ATTITUDE IS SHOWING, MacMillian Publishing

ATTITUDE: YOUR MOST PRICELESS POSSESSION, Crisp Publications, Inc.

YOUR ATTITUDE IS CHANGING, Science Research Associates

WINNING AT HUMAN RELATIONS, Crisp Publications, Inc.

BIG BUSINESS: A POSITIVE VIEW, Prentice Hall

SUPERVISOR'S SURVIVAL KIT, MacMillian Publishing

HUMAN RELATIONS IN SMALL BUSINESS, Crisp Publications, Inc.

THE NEW SUPERVISOR, Crisp Publications, Inc.

PERSONAL COUNSELING, Crisp Publications, Inc.

COMFORT ZONES: A PRACTICAL GUIDE FOR RETIREMENT PLANNING, Crisp Publications, Inc.

THE UNFINISHED BUSINESS OF LIVING, Crisp Publications, Inc.

Introduction

In 1964 I authored a book titled *Your Attitude Is Showing*. Almost thirty years and over one million copies later, the sixth edition continues to sell as well as ever. In 1986 I wrote a smaller, more personal book for the self-improvement market titled *Attitude: Your Most Priceless Possession*. It has sold well over one hundred thousand copies and was the inspiration for a training audio and video of the same name.

In asking myself why the topic of attitude has remained so popular over the years, I came to the conclusion that a positive attitude is a person's best weapon to survive in today's increasingly complex world. Those who prosper will be individuals who are able to build more upbeat perspectives for career success and personal fulfillment through a positive approach to life.

This book answers important questions raised from previous publications. It is not a rerun. Rather, *Up Your Attitude!* provides a fresh approach that explores the essence of attitude and demonstrates how staying positive improves all aspects of our lives.

Elwood N. Chapman

Contents

Contents (*Continued*)

Contents (Continued)

    (A series of questions are answered by the author)

Contents (Continued)

Chapter 1

It's Your Choice!

Chapter 1

It's Your Choice!

"Pessimists have already begun to worry about what is going to replace automation."

Laurence J. Peters

Rarely will anyone tell you outright to improve your attitude. There are several people who have thought it. But most will not tell you. Virtually everyone appreciates a person who is positive—this includes your spouse, friends, boss, co-workers and even your children. But even these individuals are reluctant to approach you on the subject directly. Why is this?

Often it is fear. People realize that attitude is one of the most sensitive parts of our personality. Our attitude is very close to our ego. It is part of our identity. Introducing the subject can be so personal that the simple mention of the word "attitude" can cause a rift in a long-term relationship. To suggest to others that they might improve their attitude could be considered an invasion of privacy. Such a suggestion could cause a response like: "Sorry, but my attitude is my business, not yours."

Despite the above, from time to time we all will have trouble with our attitudes. How then, can we feel comfortable approaching others on such a sensitive matter when our own attitude is far from perfect?

The Most Popular Word Around

Everybody uses the word attitude. You cannot go through a single day without hearing or reading about it. You hear it in conversations, on television or read about it in newspapers, books and magazines. In addition, attitude has long been a favorite word of educators and psychologists. Everybody uses it. Professional athletes are constantly being interviewed. When these stars answer questions about past or future performances, they almost always introduce the word attitude. They sometimes say that negative attitudes caused them to lose. They confess that their performance improves when their attitude is positive. Attitude seems to be a magic word in sports. And elsewhere.

The Word Nobody Fully Understands

Attitude is not only a more popular word today, it is often used in dramatic and obtuse ways. We increasingly hear people say that a person "has an attitude." Although this expression is open to many interpretations, it usually means that the individual has an attitude problem and is difficult to deal with. Or you might hear someone say "she has a new attitude that won't stop." In this case, it could mean a person has her act together and would be an interesting person to meet. There are even T-shirts that say "How's My Attitude?"

Attitude has become a "catch all" word. We resort to it when we cannot find a more definitive expression. For example, how many of the following have you heard recently?

- Someone explaining a divorce to a friend: "I just couldn't deal with his/her attitude."

- A father talking to a colleague: "Frank could be an "A" student if we could change his attitude toward school."

- One manager, talking to another, saying "she is our most capable employee, but she handicaps herself because of an attitude nobody can understand."

You can, without doubt, add numerous, similar examples.

A Textbook Definition of Attitude

Going back to basics may help us understand the word attitude. The classic textbook definition says that, *"attitude is a mental set that causes one to react to a given stimulus in a characteristic and predictable manner."* This definition indicates that we develop a larger and larger constellation or bank of mental sets that causes us to interpret what we see or sense in our environment in a predictable way. In other words, our reactions to situations are increasingly predetermined as a result of the mental sets—attitudes—we have formed.

This definition can help you understand your attitude toward specific things. It can also help you understand why you are often so stubborn about accepting change. But as good as this definition is, it is incomplete as far as knowing more about a person's *general* attitude toward life. How can people avoid developing a predetermined attitude toward all aspects of life? How can they avoid developing negative mental sets that might, eventually, turn their general attitude negative? These are difficult questions, and there are no simple answers. But there *is* a simple, direct approach that produces results. Consider this definition. It goes straight to the heart of what attitude is really all about.

A More Practical and Usable Definition

"Attitude is the way you *mentally* look at the world around you.
It is how you *view* your environment and your future. It is the
focus you develop toward life itself."

Attitude is How You Look at Things

On the surface, attitude is the way you communicate to others.
When you are optimistic and anticipate successful encounters,
you transmit a *positive way of looking at* things. When this happens, people usually respond favorably. On the other hand,
when you are pessimistic and expect the worst, you transmit a
negative way of looking at things. This is when people tend to
avoid you. Inside your head, where it all starts, *it is possible to
decide which focus you have.* Like using a camera, you can focus
your mind on what appeals to you. You can *see* situations as
either opportunities or failures. A cold winter day can be interpreted as either beautiful or depressing. A departmental meet-
ing can be viewed as interesting or boring. A remark can be taken
lightly or as an insult. A suggestion can be viewed as either helpful
or as unfair criticism. Quite simply, *you can take the pictures of
life you want to take.*

Much of the time when we use the word attitude, we would
communicate better if we simply said "he has developed a negative way of looking at things" or "she has a better way of looking
at things than she had a year ago." The more we connect attitude to the perceptual process, how we view and interpret the
world around us, the better. It does not sound very scientific,
but after thirty years of dealing with the subject, *the way you mentally look at things* remains the best definition of attitude I have
found.

What This Book Can Do For You

The objective of this book is to demonstrate that attitude is a perceptual force that can improve your life. Numerous examples

will prove that a positive focus can turn a so-so life into one that is highly exciting. A positive attitude can convert an average looking person into a beautiful one. It can make a successful person more successful. It can empower individuals to achieve goals that others consider beyond their reach. Properly understood and used, a positive attitude can enrich your personality and the impression you make on others. If you have taken the concept of attitude casually, a deeper look may cause you to change your mind and enthusiastically join the ranks of those who consider attitude to be their most priceless possession.

Why Life Itself Can Be Considered an Attitude

Life is made up of countless, ongoing stimuli, positive and negative. We interpret these stimuli in our minds, sometimes consciously—often unconsciously. The *way* we interpret what happens plays an immense role in how we live, what we enjoy and the fulfillments that life can bring. If we learn to concentrate on positive factors, we can inject more sparkle and resiliency into our lives. We can come closer to living the life we dreamed about when we were children. If, on the other hand, we focus on negatives factors, our expectations disappear and our lives turn dreary. Because it is our attitude (i.e. our mental view of things) that makes this determination, life truly can be called an attitude.

> *Gregory grew up in a negative environment. Although his family was comfortable financially, there was little joy and laughter. Instead of looking for the fun things in life, his parents were very somber. As a result, Gregory spent the first two years in college becoming increasingly critical. Most of his conversations were negative. He had few friends. Then, in an art appreciation class, he met Trish. Unlike Gregory, she focused on the good side of things. Popular and upbeat, she received invitations for all sorts of activities. Soon after they started going together, Gregory started to see the more positive and beautiful things that sur-*

rounded him. After five years, punctuated by a few separations—every now and then Gregory would resort to his negative ways—they were married.

Years later, Gregory told others: "The greatest thing that happened to me in college was not the degree I received. It was Trish. She taught me that attitude is more important than money, status, power and all the rest. Trish gave me a new perspective on life."

You Are the Guardian of Your Attitude

Nobody owns your attitude. It is exclusively yours. You alone control it. It does not belong to your employer, your family or the person you trust most. Attitude is so personal that you can even avoid talking about it. You can keep it hidden and protected. Or you can say to yourself: "Attitude controls my life, and I am going to make it work for me."

One intriguing thing about attitude is the *amount* of control you have over it. This control comes basically from the way you apply your perceptual powers. If you want to allow your mental focus to drift toward the negative factors in your environment, you will eventually miss out on many things. If, however, you decide to control your focus and ease the negative factors into the background, life can take on a totally different perspective. *All you need do is believe that what you dwell upon mentally significantly determines the state of your attitude.*

If, for example, you drive home from work and go through a congested industrial area or get caught in a traffic jam or get lost trying to avoid traffic, it is possible you have fed yourself a batch of negative stimuli. The result is that you will probably arrive home in a nasty mood. If, however, you make a conscious decision to relax and perhaps take the long way home by driving on less travelled roads, and/or playing your favorite tapes or stopping to view a sunset, you, by choice, fed your mind positive stimuli and chances are you will have a pleasant evening.

Okay, you say, but what if circumstances force you toward

negative stimuli such as the first route in the above example—is it still possible to maintain control?

Yes. Through training, you can learn to be selective and focus on positive factors that still exist. For example, you can still play your favorite tape, dream about your next holiday or turn your mental focus toward the positive factors that will be present when you reach your destination. *You still have control.*

When The Chips Are Down

Most of us do not face the world around us from a wheel chair. We live with little or no physical pain. Yet, those that do often have attitudes more positive than ours. How can this happen? It is because these people *make up their minds* to seek out and focus on the positive factors surrounding them.

Jim Porter has spent the last seven years of his life in a wheel chair or in bed. Most of the time he is in pain. Yet, he loves life and displays a positive attitude. How is he able to do this? Here is his answer, in his words: "Strange as it sounds, it is all in my mind. When I became disabled, a nurse who was helping me adjust said: 'It's your move, Jim. You can go all out and squeeze joy, happiness and fulfillment out of life, or you can atrophy. It is all in the way you decide to view your situation.' Although difficult to accept at first, I realized just how right she was and learned how to focus on the positive factors. I hope it is obvious that I chose the right road."

As you read this book, you will gain a new understanding and perspective on the importance attitude plays in your life. Even more important, you will receive techniques and strategies on how to control your attitude. If you eventually decide that life is pretty much a matter of what you want to perceive, you will be on a winning track. And you will know, from that point forward, that you have found the key to a better life.

Chapter 2

The Inside Scoop!

Chapter 2

The Inside Scoop!

"Your mind is a sacred enclosure into which nothing harmful can enter except by your permission."
                                        Arnold Bennet

Perception is the process whereby we view and interpret the culture in which we live. It usually starts as a visual matter and then turns into a mental process. We see with our eyes, but we interpret with all five senses. Taste, touch, smell and hearing also play an important role.

The actual process of interpretation is too complex to understand. Psychologists have spent lifetimes working on perceptual theories they are unable to universally prove. Often these theories are not communicated clearly to the rest of us. Part of the dilemma is that interpretation is *selective*. A human can, for the most part, accept, diminish, explain, justify or reject stimuli from the outside world. In other words, there is no clear understanding about why people do not give equal attention to both positive and negative factors.

Pat lived her first twenty years after high school knowing she was not living up to her potential. She blamed her ex-husband, her ex-bosses, and members of her family for her failures. Then one day a friend who had known her for over ten years said: "Pat, you keep blaming the world around you for your unhappiness. Why don't you look inside at your own attitude? Frankly, you are so negative I often feel depressed after being with you."

The result? Pat was able to develop a selectivity process which she calls "scan and sift." In an effort to be more upbeat, she has learned to scan, or perceive, the stimuli she must deal with each day and sift, or divert, annoying negatives away from her mental concentration so the remaining positives "make her day."

Pat now tells people: "For years I fell into the trap of concentrating on negatives, and I was miserable. Then, thanks to a friend, I learned to sift out the garbage and concentrate on the roses. Believe me, you would not have wanted to know me in those days."

Perceptual Field Explained

What people see and interpret is their perceptual field. Each individual's perceptions are unique. Their perceptions are composed of countless factors or elements which interact. To simplify and understand the concept of attitude, it is necessary to break factors into two groups—those with the power to lift one's spirits and those that pull spirits down. A plus charge comes from positive factors—a minus from negative. To maintain an upbeat perspective, it is vital to concentrate on, and react to, positive factors and keep those with negative impact to a minimum. It is possible for you to accomplish this through mental discipline, a learned behavior, and several other techniques which will be discussed later in this book.

Positive Factors   **Negative Factors**

Perceptual Field Visualized

The circle below will help you to *visualize* a perceptual field. It must be recognized that this effort is simply a graphic representation and is an over-simplification. There are probably no acceptable physical or psychological foundations or theories upon which to build such an approach. This illustration, and those to follow, are for *communication purposes only.*

View the circle below as a hypothetical representation that contains, at any moment, a perceptual field (mental focus on life) that could belong to anybody.

A BALANCED PERCEPTUAL FIELD

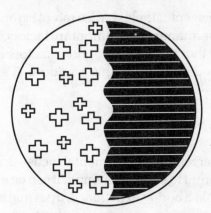

You will notice that there are plus signs on one side of the circle and minus signs on the other. The plus signs represent factors that give you a lift. The minus signs represent items that can pull a dark cloud over your focus. The illustration is elementary, but it makes a significant point.

To put yourself into this plus or minus process, you are encouraged to list the five most positive and the five most negative factors in your life today. Think about and then select those that consume the largest portion of your mind-time.

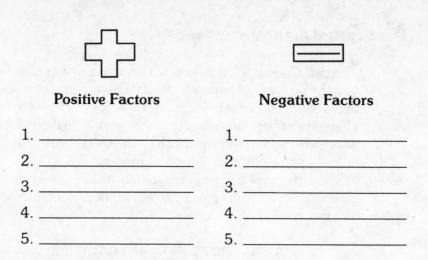

Positive Factors   **Negative Factors**

1. _____   1. _____

2. _____   2. _____

3. _____   3. _____

4. _____   4. _____

5. _____   5. _____

All perceptual fields have a mix of big and small, real and imaginary, permanent and temporary factors. Notice in our first illustration that the plus and minus factors are equally divided or balanced. In real life, this is seldom, if ever, the case.

Your Perceptual Field

Your perceptual field—mental focus—includes everything that you permit to enter your mind. It can be a sunny day, an intriguing book, a boring experience, a pet that brings you joy, or a person who you do not completely trust. All perceptual fields contain negative factors. For example, you might take a dream vacation in which all factors are positive until you run into a nasty desk clerk or miss a flight. Or, you might buy your dream home and then discover you have a neighbor whose son has frequent, loud parties. Only in a dream world is it possible to eliminate all negative factors from life.

Concentration Is the Key

As long as we must live with negatives, and we must, the best strategy we can employ is to learn how to concentrate or keep our focus on the positives. By giving upbeat factors increased "mind-time," we can learn to bring them center stage so they will make life more positive.

> *Sid is considered by those who know him best as a "worrier." Whenever his mind is idle, Sid permits it to focus on little things that might go wrong but probably will not. For example, Sid worries excessively about whether he is carrying enough insurance on his car and personal possessions, whether his tires are getting too worn, whether he will be late for work, and so on. As a result, Sid magnifies potential negatives instead of taking advantage of his existing positives. Sid could reduce his worrying time by focusing on the good things in his life. The more he concentrates and expands on positives, the less "worry time" will be available for either real or potential negatives.*

Positive and Negative Perceptual Fields

Sometimes outside stimuli are so negative and problems become so overwhelming that positive factors can become temporarily buried. For example, you could be cruising along in a happy mood, feeling things are going your way, only to discover one day, in a surprise announcement at work, that your job has been eliminated. Although you will get severance pay, you quickly realize that a major adjustment lies ahead. This is a period when all sorts of negatives start to surface in your thoughts. Will you be able to find a job to match the one eliminated? Will you be able to make the payments on your new car? What lifestyle changes will be necessary? Will you have to move? Your focus on life might look like this:

NEGATIVE PERCEPTUAL FIELD

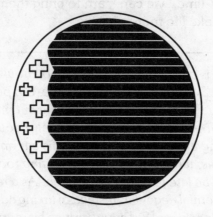

On the other hand, sometimes positives can overwhelm even major negatives. For example, you might have permitted yourself to become negative because you have been passed over several times for a promotion. You have become discouraged. Then, out of the blue comes a new career opportunity that you have always wanted, with a competitor. Your spirits and confidence soar. All of a sudden you are back focusing on positives and, because of your new attitude, things are getting better and better. Your discouraging days are over.

POSITIVE PERCEPTUAL FIELD

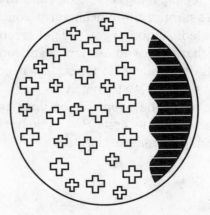

We All Have the Same Challenge

In real life, despite the highs and lows, sooner or later a more balanced distribution of negatives and positives returns and, once again, you must work to keep the focus on the positives.

> *Reverend Walker, a Protestant minister, has a positive attitude that has enabled him and his wife to double the size of their congregation in five years. Still, he admits that each week is a new challenge. "I start out on Monday feeling "down" and have to fight with myself all week to recover my focus so I am prepared for Sunday. It is then that I reach my "peak." I guess Monday is a natural let-down and renewal period for me. I've never figured it out. The challenge would be twice as hard if it were not for my wife. I may be the ordained minister, but she's the one with the positive attitude."*

Everyone has trouble staying positive. It is part of being human. Remaining in focus is our number one, life long, challenge. That is why each of us must develop a strategy to push negative factors to the outer perimeter of our thinking. We will, of course, do this in our own style.

ACCEPTING THE CHALLENGE

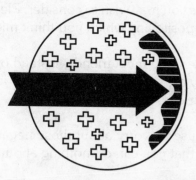

> *Whenever Denise finds she is concentrating excessively on a few negative factors that are currently plaguing her life, she plays a game with herself. She moves to the positive side of her perceptual field and selects **three** postive factors in her life. She writes them down on a small piece of paper that she places in her billfold. Denise then decides she will use any free mind-time remaining in the day to concentrate on the most important of the three. She seldom gets to number two or three.*

Denise is using mental discipline to stay positive. In a way, she is setting aside or cancelling the negatives in her perceptual field in favor of the positives.

> *Gregg claims he has discovered a way to wake up in the morning with a more positive attitude. His technique is to replay each day in his mind after turning out the light to go to sleep. **But he only deals with positive factors.** Gregg feels he sleeps better and, upon waking the next morning, his mind often replays the positive events of the previous day so that his attitude — perceptual field — is in better focus.*

Some Techniques to Help You Stay Positive

Those who succeed in keeping their focus primarily on positive employ many personal techniques. Listed below are a few suggestions you may wish to consider. Please place a check mark (✔) opposite any which you think might work for you.

☐ When you meet friends, instead of asking them "how they are doing," ask them to tell you the bright spot of their day.

☐ Refuse to worry about those negative elements in your life that you can do nothing about.

☐ Do not borrow negative factors from other people by trying to live their lives for them. You have all you can handle keeping your own focus positive.

☐ Save a few minutes each day to visualize your perceptual field (circle), so you can see what adjustments need to be made.

☐ Dispose of small, nagging problems quickly by addressing them. Take care of bigger problems by breaking them into smaller components that can be solved.

☐ When anticipating what lies ahead in a day, think about the good things that can happen.

☐ When replaying the events of a day, think about your accomplishments.

☐ Share what you are learning about attitude with the person you care the most about.

☐ Talk openly to this same person about the state of your attitude.

☐ Add your own.

_____

_____

_____

Imaging and a More Positive Attitude

A survey of research on the subject of "mental imaging" turned up three suggestions that are applicable to achieving a more positive attitude. These suggestions are:

1. *To a limited extent, what we envision in life is what we get.* Translated as far as maintaining a positive attitude is concerned, this means the more we perceive positives and ignore negatives the better. Visualizing a perceptual field (circle) is a device that can help bring this about.

2. *An image can be a self-fulfilling prophecy.* When we create positive images or enhance existing positive factors, we improve our chances of becoming more positive. Here again, visualizing the process through a graphic can be helpful.

3. *To cause something positive to happen, we must REALLY want what we visualize.* A deep emotional commitment is necessary.

The perceptual field approach prescribed and recommended in this book is a form of imaging. As you construct your mental picture of your personal perceptual field, using the graphics as models, you are engaging yourself in the process of imaging. Building upon the visuals presented, you can learn how and when to focus your mind for maximum results. Each positive factor within your perceptual field can be brought to life and enhanced.

Ideally, the image you create will serve the additional purpose of acting as a reminder that now and then your attitude is showing and it is time to refocus and concentrate on the positives.

Do Whatever it Takes to Magnify the Positive and Diffuse the Negative

Emphasizing the positive and diffusing the negative is like using a magnifying glass. You can place the glass over good news and feel better, or you can magnify bad news and make yourself miserable. Magnifying unpleasant or problem situations can become a habit. If you continually focus on difficult factors, the result is usually an exaggerated distortion. A better approach might be to imagine you have binoculars. Use the magnifying end to view positive factors; reverse the binoculars, using the other end, on negative elements to make them appear smaller. No matter how you do it, once you alter your imagery to magnify the positive, you are on the right track.

Chapter 3

Negative Drift

Negative Drift

> *"The optimist proclaims that we live in the best of all possible worlds, and the pessimist fears this is true."*
>
> *James Branch Cabell*

Observation and hundreds of interviews dealing with the subject of attitude for over forty years has convinced me that there is a subtle but consistent pressure that pushes a dark film over our perceptual fields. The movement has the tendency to cover up the positive and highlight the negative.

NEGATIVE DRIFT

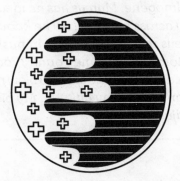

This phenomenon, for lack of a better label, is called *negative drift*. Similar to a pall of black smoke that hides a sunny landscape, negative drift is a gloomy cloud that prevents us from seeing many of the positive factors in our lives. Unless we create a positive force in the opposite direction (see chapter 2), negative factors soon take over and dominate our perceptual fields. We begin to think negatively, talk negatively and our lives turn dull. We lose our normal, positive spark.

Imogene's Focus

Imogene enjoyed a successful career as a dental hygienist for ten years before she fell in love with Roberto. She presently spends her time at home raising their three children. She is satisifed with her role, but every now and then a blue curtain falls over her perspective, and she misses the old days when she was free, had adult contacts during the day and could go out at night. To fight off the negative overlay, Imogene resorts to many techniques. So far, the most successful has been to focus on a goal of returning to her profession in two years when their youngest child enters pre-school. She and Roberto talk the plan over frequently and she knows he is behind her 100 percent.

Unlike Imogene, Marcus has no idea what pulls the negative film across his focus. All he knows is that when it happens he is usually successful in pushing it back by riding his motorcycle on some country roads. "It's strange, but the speed and the wind seem to blow negative feelings away and I can refocus my attitude. My bike is my primary attitude adjuster."

Assume, for a moment, that you are in a mental state where there are no major negatives in your life. Your health is good, money is not a serious problem, you have good, solid relationships, you like your job, you enjoy your family and you have a variety of friends. In other words, everything is great.

BEFORE NEGATIVE DRIFT

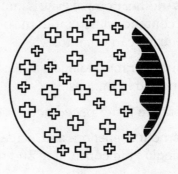

Under ideal conditions, such as those described, can negative drift occur? Unfortunately, the answer is "yes." Negative drift is above and beyond any specific negative factors that are in our perceptual fields. It is, in some respects, a separate phenomenon—a superimposed mood that has no easily identifiable cause. Negative drift does not eliminate positives, but it can cast a negative film over one's focus, so that even a fortunate person's perspective becomes negative.

AFTER NEGATIVE DRIFT

Causes of Negative Drift

Have you ever had a discussion over whether it is more difficult to stay positive today than in the past? One party may claim that his or her parents and grandparents had just as many troubles as we do. Another point of view is that there are more negative factors to contend with in modern society. The person taking this perspective can point to:

- More drugs, crime, violence, traffic and litigation today than at any period in the past

- Jobs that are faster paced and more stressful

- Government regulations and increased bureaucracy that are increasingly time consuming and complex

- Television that provides an overdose of negative images and violence—through repetition, the media has a way of hammering the negative more deeply into our minds. Networks claim "good news is boring."

Consider two old friends who have worked out a solution to reduce television's negative drift. Together, they evaluate what television shows, movies and plays they view based upon whether the experience will be educational, humorous or otherwise positive. They conclude anything educational or humorous will improve their perspective—but that other stimuli is suspect. After discussing each opportunity, they make a joint decision. As you might expect, they favor educational and family programming.

With so many social and economic problems surfacing around the world, a good question becomes: "How can anyone today be an informed citizen, make a contribution to a better world, and still remain positive?" One answer lies in understanding our perceptions. For example, if we learn to concentrate on what *remains* positive, while we work on correcting negatives, it is possible to make progress. This is not an easy challenge.

Is Negative Drift a Natural Phenomenon?

If you are a person who downplays contemporary negatives, perhaps you agree with the premise that negative drift is a natural, human condition, and it has always been present. For example, many individuals seem to have an inclination or disposition to accept and occasionally favor negatives over positives. *Some people seem to relish bad news.* One wonders if some individuals, either consciously or unconsciously, create their own negative drift.

> *Carol is considered by her co-workers to be an information magnet. They have unofficially designated her as the manager of the company rumor mill and supervisor of the grapevine. Carol discovered years ago that one way to gain attention was to spread intriguing but negative gossip. She did not take into consideration, however, that her emphasis on negatives would cause her to lose the respect of both co-workers and management. Even more significant, her negative talk infiltrated her own psyche and caused her to be a negative person, both at work and at home.*

What other factors may be involved in creating negative drift? Certainly such issues as a person's early home environment and the absence of positive role models could be responsible for a disposition that is inherently more negative. Or perhaps it could be a biological predilection. Who can tell? The important thing, of course, is that each individual, to a certain degree, come to grips with her/his personal negative drift. The greater the drift, the more an opposing force is needed.

> *Aaron grew up in a negative home environment. He became a "loner" until he was in high school. Then, his only friend introduced him to the guitar, and Aaron discovered he had a talent for music. Within weeks he was playing contemporary songs by ear. During his senior year he started to play and sing at parties. The change in his attitude — from negative to positive — was obvous to everyone. When asked about the change, Aaron said: "Every time I begin*

to withdraw, I pick up my guitar and start playing. Music helps me to see life in a more positive way."

Hank thinks a lot about life. He realizes that he has strong negative tendencies, even though he has no serious problems. For reasons he does not understand, he is more irritable and reactionary than others to events. The good news is that Hank is able to compensate. He constantly builds up the positive factors in his life, including his self-image. Result? He talks positively, he thinks positively, and the end result is that other people think Hank is an unusually positive person.

Carla views her tendency to swing in the direction of the negative as a mental "handicap" that she has learned to overcome. Knowing that her negative drift applies constant pressure on her positive focus, she has developed mechanisms to keep it pushed back. For example, the moment Carla senses a negative cloud on the horizon, she invites an upbeat friend to lunch, takes a ride in the country, or makes a long-distance call to a special family member. Recognizing her weakness has helped Carla successfully deal with the phenomenon in the beginning stages. She believes in prevention instead of major surgery later.

A Counterforce is Needed to Combat Negative Drift

If you agree there is such a thing as negative drift, you will also probably agree that a strong counterforce is necessary.

The problem intensifies when we recognize that an opposing force must be sufficiently powerful to hold back negative drift
as well as deal with actual negative elements already within an
individual's perceptual field. Under these conditions, remaining "upbeat" can be a magnificent achievement.

> *Evelyn had come to understand and deal effectively with
> her natural tendencies toward negative drift, even before
> her serious accident. Now, with an artificial leg, she has to
> fight ten times as hard to maintain her positive focus. How
> is she doing? She is doing well. Her therapists were able
> to restore her perspective at a higher level. Today it is appar-
> ent that Evelyn has grown into a new role. She is an inspi-
> ration to those lucky enough to know her. When asked how
> she managed the transition, she replies: "It is nothing more
> than attitude — pure attitude. When the chips were down,
> I was forced to call upon my inner resources to survive."*

Reflect for a moment and select the most consistently positive person you know. Choose this individual from anyone you
have ever known, at work or in your personal life. Now ask yourself this question: Does my choice have to *work* at staying positive? Chances are the answer is "yes." Few people are endowed
with a positive attitude that does not require great inner strength
to maintain. If possible, to check your choice, invite the person
you selected to have a cup of coffee or tea, and ask them directly
how they are able to project such a positive outlook. Then ask
if they have to work at it. Chances are that almost 100 percent
will answer "yes!"

Everybody has the potential to be positive, but it does not
come easily. Self-awareness, mental discipline and, most of all,
meaningful goals are necessary to keep the constant pressure
of negative drift at bay. Even when people have few negatives
in their lives, they must continue to employ the same techniques
and strategies that others less fortunate use to keep negative drift
from taking over. Just a little carelessness, and you lose ground.

Questions That Need to be Answered

Whether you agree or disagree on the presence of negative drift, certain things take on new significance when the idea is discussed. Here are a few questions that require answers:

- Must we conduct a day-to-day psychological war to keep negative factors from dominating our lives?

- Without developing a sufficiently strong counterforce, are we destined to drift toward the negative? If so, then does not having a positive life goal or purpose take on a new meaning?

- Should the concept of negative drift send a signal to management that all working environments need to be more lively, humorous and positive to keep the negatives from taking over and damaging productivity?

- Do we need to take a new look at how we use the media, so that we can stay informed without being overdosed with negative reporting and/or "entertainment"?

- How much idleness and inactivity can a person enjoy without opening the doors to negative drift?

- Do people who either insulate or isolate themselves from the negatives in our environment create and sustain a more positive attitude than do others?

Every person will answer such questions differently. The purpose of introducing negative drift has not been to discourage you, but rather to present the full dimensions of what attitude is about. Until the challenge is understood, you cannot win the game.

Chapter 4

The Mental Health Connection

Chapter 4

The Mental Health Connection

> *"A person must try to worry about things that aren't important so he won't worry too much about things that are."*
>
> **Jack Smith**

We use the word attitude to communicate aspects of wellness; yet, strange as it may seem, we seldom seem to connect attitude with mental health. This is a mistake because attitude is a terrific barometer of mental health. When a person's focus is composed of mainly positives, we can safely say the individual's mental health is excellent. When the opposite is true, we can claim the individual's mental health is not so good.

Mental Health Defined

Mental health is the ability to work, love and play with relative freedom from internal stress. When things get tough on the outside, mental health is the capacity to cope on the inside. Most medical experts agree that mental health is as important to the holistic concept of wellness as physical health. We exercise and watch our diets to stay in top physical health. We join health clubs, buy exercise equipment and take pride in our bodies. But what about mental health? What can we do to stay mentally fit?

> *At 42, Warren was physically fit, due to a regular exercise regime and a carefully monitored diet. However, when his*

wife demanded he sign divorce papers and move out, he was devastated to the point that he neglected his exercise and diet. After a few months, Warren's wellness factor was low and getting lower. A friend with whom he had worked out in prior years persuaded Warren to join a singles group sponsored by a local fitness center. Through open communication, centered around the trauma of separation and recovery strategies and a group exercise program, Warren regained his positive focus and returned to his previous state of wellness. In the process, he learned that mental health and attitude are clearly connected to the exercise and diet sides of "wellness."

Creating and maintaining an upbeat attitude plays a major role in staying mentally healthy. When we focus on the positives, we ride high on the mental health barometer. We relate well with others, produce above average results in our jobs, and have more fun. In this frame of mind, we can face problems with more inner strength and find better solutions. Just as people who take good care of their physical bodies are in better shape to face a major operation, those who develop positive attitudes are in better shape to face down periods of stress or depression. Having prepared themselves, they can usually bounce back more readily.

Working Through Major Problems

When an unexpected and traumatic event occurs in our lives, it is normal for the negative side of our perceptual field to take over and crowd out the positive. Today, when people face serious difficulties, we hear them say they are "working through" the problem.

> *"Sorry Sally, I won't be able to take the trip with you. I am working my way **through** a career problem."*

*"Without the help of my counselor, it would have taken me years to work **through** my problem."*

Working through is an excellent expression, providing the person involved is aware that one must re-strengthen old and create new positives during the "working through" period. Put another way, the process means leaving some negative factors behind and expanding factors on the positive side of our perceptual field. Here are two examples:

With a well above-average annual income, Sally had nevertheless allowed herself to get deeply into debt. After looking into the possibility of a consolidation loan, she saw, for the first time, the depth of the financial hole she had dug. She talked the problem over with Vi, her friend, who said, "Sally, you have two problems, not one. First, you've got to work yourself out of debt. This may take two or three years. Second, you've got to work through this experience without letting it get to your attitude and damage your career. You can do it, but you will have to change your spending habits and lifestyle. For what it is worth, I think a positive attitude is more important than a good credit rating."

When Roland agreed to have open-heart surgery, he tried to have a cavalier attitude. "Just one of those things," he would say. But deep inside he knew it was a major turning point in his life. It would mean a new diet, a daily exercise program, and a more controlled existence. What he did not anticipate was the need to make a career change and some tough financial adjustments. Two years later, in talking to a close friend, Roland said: "I now know what it means to work **through** a problem now. My biggest struggle was my attitude, now feel I have everything under control but my golf game."

Is It Mentally Healthy to Create Positive Illusions?

Good news! There is something else we can do to build up the positive side of our perceptual fields. It may not appeal to everyone, but, to me, it is an important break-through as far as attitude and mental health are concerned.

Dr. Shelly Taylor, a Social Psychologist at U.C.L.A., has done some outstanding research in this area. In her book *Positive Illusions** she supports the concept that a healthy mind is able to ward off negative information and concentrate on positive factors. She also adds that creating a few positive illusions improves the process. This means that creating a few fantasies or "dreams" and inserting them into the positive side of your perceptual field can accentuate the positive and enhance your life. A few of these make-believe factors can be as important as some of your positive reality factors.

Positive Illusions Defined

A positive illusion is a fanciful vision of the conscious mind. Although conceived by the mind, the vision need not exist in reality. When we hear the expression "he seems to be living in a dream world," we should not be critical. Perhaps the individual cannot find enough positive factors in his perceptual field, so he creates some. Perhaps this is the way the individual maintains a positive attitude.

Most people indulge in fantasies. Here is an example:

> *John grew up in Texas where he really wanted to be a cowboy, but turned out to be an engineer. For over 40 years he has read Western novels to satisfy his childhood fantasy. One evening, in talking about the past with a friend, John said: "Maybe I was born 50 years too late, but at least*

* *Basic Books,* Sub-division, Harper & Row Publications, 10 E. 53rd Street, New York, NY 10022, 1989

I can fantasize about the past so I neutralize the stress of modern life. That's the best thing about reading. It is possible to live two lives. The one you imagine helps you keep a more positive view of the present. At least that's the way I see it."

Using Imaging to Speed Up a Recovery

Imaging can be interpreted as the process of creating an illusion in which you play a winning role. It is a mental technique designed to expand the positive side of one's perceptual field.

Assume that your doctor has determined that you have a serious illness and prescribes medicine that may or may not correct the problem. After giving instructions on how often to take the medication, your doctor states: "Your attitude can have something to do with the speed and success of your recovery. The more you imagine and anticipate a full recovery, the better."

You do a little research and discover how imaging might help.

Possibility 1:
If you visualize that the illness you have consists of tiny little enemies bent on destroying you and the medicine is tiny little victory fighters who can save you, you are engaging in imaging. The technique is to take the pills as prescribed, and then picture them attacking and defeating the enemy force, thus gaining your normal good health back. The idea is that your mind is giving the medicine a better chance to help you.

Possibility 2:
You decide you can give the medicine a boost by visualizing a "party" you will give yourself once your recovery is complete. The celebration you plan need not be a realistic one. It can be totally imaginary but nevertheless translates into a goal. The idea is that by projecting yourself into a state of health that would allow you to participate in such an event, you will make the medicine more effective.

Attitude is a powerful force and most people believe that it is an important factor in helping many people recover their previous state of health.

INSERTING POSITIVE ILLUSIONS

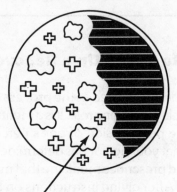

Inserting positive illusions into one's perceptual field is a mental process that can be initiated by design.

Positive Illusions Help Defeat Negatives

When we create positive illusions to keep the positive elements in our perceptual fields ahead of the negative, we are improving our mental health. We need not apologize for our efforts.

To an outsider, June appears to have more negatives in her life than positives. She lives alone, has a routine accounting job, does little traveling, and has a severe hearing problem. But June does not look at her life that way. She feels the positives far outweigh the negatives. How can this be? Because June is a constant reader and always puts herself into the roles of the most interesting characters. In other words, through reading, she creates a stream of posi-

tive illusions to balance out the negatives in her life, over which she has no control. She also belongs to a local theater group where she plays "bit parts."

It has been one blow after another for Jason. Due to a hostile take-over, he lost his job. Then he lost his wife to cancer. Jason's life is full of negatives, yet he continues to be upbeat. How does he compensate? Jason has always had a deep interest in the sea, so he creates sea-faring illusions that substitute for real-life adventures. He also has become involved with Sea Scouts, which permits him to help maintain a boat, work with navigational instruments, and take an occasional trip out of the marina near his home.

Like June and Jason, it is mentally healthy for us to conjure up "dream" trips, give ourselves celebrity status, imagine romantic encounters, and satisfy a range of unfulfilled desires in our minds. But, best of all, the negative reality factors we face are seen in a better perspective because illusions can provide us with a few positive factors to help us improve our focus.

Sometimes, to deal with reality effectively, we need to channel our minds to positive illusions that will balance out the severity of the negative factors. We need to do this because, at this point, there are not enough real positives to compensate.

Barry, a widower whose activities are restricted due to a leg injury, has accumulated over 100 video cassettes of his favorite movies. An outstanding dancer in earlier years, Barry's favorite videos are musicals with Fred Astaire and Gene Kelly. When Barry needs to manufacture a positive to add to his perceptual field, he turns to a musical, pretends he is young again and dances in his memory with June Powell and others. Barry makes excellent use of his VCR and is more positive because of it. He also makes many friends by loaning videos out to others.

Positive Illusions and Dealing with Reality Problems

Do people who indulge heavily in illusions pay a price when they must face difficult reality problems? Do they sometimes walk away and leave the responsibility to others? Perhaps, but there is no strong evidence this happens for the vast majority. Of course, if an individual carries the practice too far, it can be a problem. We have all heard about reclusives and/or alcoholics who have retreated from reality. Most people, however, strike a balance between positives and negatives that *helps* them solve problems.

Cedric leads a hectic life as a lawyer in a major city. From early Monday until late Friday, he, his secretary and two paralegals face one crisis after another. To compensate, each Saturday morning Cedric, his wife and their dog head for a hide away on a lake, 80 miles away. There, they lead a life of seclusion and fantasy. No television, no newspapers, no telephone. Cedric, a naturalist at heart, walks in the wilderness areas, writes a little poetry and pretends he lives in an earlier time. His wife paints. In their minds, they are living two lives — one reality, one fantasy. Cedric feels the two complement each other.

Create Your Own Illusions

Below are five possible advantages to creating some positive illusions. Check whether you agree or disagree.

Agree   Disagree

☐   ☐   If I create a few illusions to add to the positive side of my perceptual field, it will make it easier for me to face the negative realities of my life.

☐   ☐   If I engage in a hobby (woodworking, model making, crafts, sewing, etc.), keeping my hands busy will free my mind and encourage me to dream. This, in turn, will help my attitude.

☐   ☐   If reality opens the floodgates to the negative side of my perceptual field, resorting to illusions can help me get back to the positive side.

☐   ☐   As long as I do not over-do it, living in two worlds can make me more productive in my career.

☐   ☐   In a world of confusion and increasing negatives, a few illusions can help me maintain better mental health.

Goals Are Involved

Later in this book, we will show just how critical goal-setting is to maintaining a positive perspective. For now, it is important to realize that we all have individual ways of constructing illusions and goals to keep the positive side of our perceptual fields strong, healthy and vibrantly alive:

• Gwen turns to music when she wishes to give her positive factors a lift.

- Dixie turns to poetry to push back the negative factors in his perceptual field.

- Art turns to nature to sustain his mental health.

- Frances turns to recalling athletic achievements to keep a positive perspective.

- Joe turns to "clowning" to keep negative factors under control.

- Cynthia turns to romantic fantasies to keep her positive views.

Everyone who stays mentally healthy eventually designs an individualized strategy to keep positive factors in focus.

If creating a few positive illusions helps in this process, then the individual should be encouraged to continue the practice as long as reality factors receive first priority.

Chapter 5

Relationships

Relationships

> *"Love doesn't make the world go 'round. Love is what makes the ride worthwhile."*
>
> Franklin P. Jones

Relationships Are Positive Or Negative

Relationships have the potential to be beautiful. Good relationships are perhaps the most basic factor in the quality of a person's life. Attitude is often the deciding factor in the success of any relationship. For example, two individuals can fall in love and remain positives in the perceptual field of the other for years. However, unfortunately, the opposite can also be true. The reality is that unless a person makes a major effort to maintain a relationship, it has the potential to deteriorate like poor health, financial set-backs, or career problems.

There is no question that those people most important to us hold a powerful influence on our attitudes. You can probably identify those who expand the positive side of your perception, and those who expand the negative. To personalize this view, please list three people who currently have a positive impact on your attitude and three who are causing you to have a more negative focus:

Positive	Negative
_____	_____
_____	_____
_____	_____

Negative Relationships

Now ask yourself these questions about your negative choices:

1. Are you being fair to those listed above whom you claim are having a negative influence on your life?

2. Is there open and frequent communication between both parties?

3. Is the negative relationship doing as much or more damage to the other individual as it is doing to you?

4. As long as the relationship remains in your perceptual field, is there a chance of moving it back to the positive side?

Relationship Defined

A relationship is most simply defined as "feelings" between two people. Some relationships have sexual overtones, most do not. When feelings are positive, relationships contain high levels of love, trust, respect or admiration. We call these significant relationships. They are uplifting and meaningful to both individuals.

It is not easy to maintain healthy, positive, long-standing relationships because two key factors must be continuously present. First, honest and free communication must take place on a regular basis. *Communication is the life blood of any significant relationship.* Without water, flowers dry up and die; without communication, individuals drift apart and the relationship dies. You will recognize the following because you have probably been there yourself.

> *Jessie and Sue have had a falling out over a trivial matter. Jess has refused to call Sue for two weeks. He mistakenly feels silence will cause her to come around to his way of thinking. Sue, on the other hand, thinks it is important for her to take a stand. Neither is willing to take the initiative*

> *to set up a meeting to talk things out and dissipate the mis-understanding. Result? They are in danger of losing a good relationship.*

    Second, the relationship must be mutually rewarding. That is, both parties must benefit from the association. When this happens, each individual is in a position to help the other maintain a more positive frame of mind or attitude. Instead of a losing situation, it becomes a win-win arrangement. Here is a classic case.

> *George was so eager to climb the corporate ladder to provide the best possible lifestyle for his family, he failed to recognize that they needed his personal involvement as well. Along with possessions, his wife needed recognition. Along with home and community amenities, his children needed personal growth in many directions. George was trying to be a good husband and father. It was not the absence of rewards, he just was not encouraging and providing the **right** rewards.*

    In every relationship that remains healthy, both parties must receive somewhat equal rewards. Each must grow. Both must win as separate identities. And finally, each must help the other gain a more positive outlook.

Avoiding Negative Tilts to Your Focus

    With close and meaningful relationships, one party can have either a supporting or a devastating impact upon the attitude of the other.

When Joel had a positive relationship with his supervisor, he was enthusiastic about his job and career future. When the relationship deteriorated over an incident where both individuals were at fault, Joel turned bitter and his negative attitude kept him from enjoying his job and making progress. Eventually he resigned.

When Frank discovered he had diabetes, he did not want to see anybody. Six months later, he knew that Donna had emerged as the one person with whom he could communicate freely and depend upon. A year later, after Frank had made a full adjustment to his illness, he knew she would be the most positive influence on his attitude for the rest of his life. Donna felt the same way. Their marriage was a big event!

Jewel thought she and Dan could have a friendly divorce. But when the settlement was finally signed, the inner conflict that had been there all along surfaced and they became open adversaries. Dan turned out to be a negative in Jewel's life. Jewel became a negative in Dan's. The freedom both wanted turned out to be bittersweet until both were able to push the negative impact of their divorce into the past. Neither party anticipated that the breakup would victimize both parties.

Protecting Your Positive Attitude from Damaged Relationships

Relationships that do not work out often catapult one from the positive to the negative side of a person's perceptual field overnight. Positive factors disappear as the new negative joins others previously under control.

The following simple suggestions can help you maintain more healthy, supportive relationships and, at the same time, provide "damage control" should a significant relationship fall apart.

Suggestion 1:

Appreciate the positive relationships you already possess. The easiest thing in the world is to lose a treasured relationship because you took it for granted. We need to be constantly aware that it makes no sense to go it alone in life. We need others to bolster our attitude when it becomes negative. We need to surround ourselves with some strong relationships that will become our support system when it is most needed.

> *Drake counted seven key people in his support system. His mother, his wife, their two children (both in college) and three close friends. Each makes a positive contribution to Drake's daily life. In turn, he keeps in close communication with all. Result? When Drake feels "down" he can get on the telephone with one or more of the seven for an attitude "booster shot."*

We all have a personal support system. This does not mean we cannot have other important relationships. We can. It simply means that we are more dependent on a few key people to maintain our positive focus and these individuals deserve special attention.

Suggestion 2:

Shift shaky relationships back to the positive side. When it comes to maintaining fragile relationships, we all make our share of mistakes. Sometimes we are neglectful. At other times we unintentionally offend. And often we are unforgiving over mistakes that others make. On occasion a "conflict" develops and we suddenly find what used to be a positive relationship is now a negative one. We have been hurt. We are fed up. We permit the broken relationship to use up our mind-time and drag our attitudes down. Sometimes we even seek revenge.

> Neither Clara nor her daughter Meg knew exactly why they had drifted apart. Was it lack of communication, a misunderstanding over childhood days or were they blaming each other because their lives had not turned out the way they had planned? Anyway, Clara knew Meg was down because her job had turned sour, so she invited her to take a vacation at a beach house. After a week together, talking over both the good and the bad times of the past, they were able to restore their relationship to its previous level. In short, they both put their relationship with each other back on the positive side of their focus and, in so doing, improved their attitudes.

Suggestion 3:
Shrink the influence that old, worn-out relationships have on your positive attitude. Not all relationships can be saved. Some become so destructive to both parties that the only solution is to abandon them and move on. In other words, what was once positive has turned hopelessly negative and each party victimizes himself or herself by permitting it to stay alive.

> Betty will never forgive Christy for pulling Jeff away from her. Betty and Jeff had been living together for over two years when Christy and Betty became co-workers and good friends.
>
> Then, at a party where Christy was her guest, Betty introduced Christy to Jeff. Two months later Betty discovered that Jeff and Christy were secretly going out and the whole thing blew up. To this day, both Jeff and Christy are time-consuming negatives in Betty's life.

If you allow any relationship to move from a plus to a minus in your perceptual field, it will, in all likelihood, occupy excessive mind-time and *you will become a victim*. We have all heard about romances that have fallen apart for someone, and that individual has subsequently carried the effect of the damage for the rest of his or her life—blocking out the possibility of an even better replacement relationship. Who is hurt the most when this happens? Who is the *real* victim? The answer is clearly the person who carried the negative around as excess baggage. Ultimately, the individual became needlessly negative.

Carrying a grudge or a resentment—even if you have clearly been deceived by another—is an attitude depressant. If you cannot forget what happened, if you cannot wipe it out of your mind, the only thing left is to reduce it to the smallest possible size so that it will not have an undue and unnecessary influence upon your positive focus.

When a Relationship Ends

Consider these possibilities when a relationship ends:

- Virtually all psychologists claim that it is best to talk a problem or loss out of your system instead of trying to bury it inside.

- When a relationship is over, discipline your mind to remember the good times, instead of replaying the bad times.

- If appropriate, find a positive substitute for the lost relationship.

- Discover a new interest or goal that will occupy your mind and give you something positive to think about, talk about and accomplish.

Studies of older adults have shown that some widows or widowers do a far better job of adjusting to their losses than others.

When Maxine lost her husband of 42 years, she might have converted her loss into a giant negative. She had observed a few of her friends doing this very thing. Fortunately for Maxine, she and her late husband Fred had talked about life after the death of the other. The essence of the plan was simply to appreciate the positive years they had enjoyed together and to continue to build a rewarding life. In short, honor the departed partner by continuing to live and grow.

How did it work out for Maxine? After the initial adjustment, she was able to focus on good memories about Fred. Then, she found a new community project and put her energy into it. Finally, she started to accept invitations from other men to go out socially. It was not easy, but by concentrating on new positives, she was able to continue building a rewarding life for herself.

Human Relations Skills Make the Difference

You cannot dismiss the importance of human relation skills in maintaining a viable support group. The more friends you develop, the more positives there are in your focus. The longer you keep a friend, the more significance his or her influence will have on your attitude.

Often, when people retire, they may or may not miss the work aspects of their previous job, but they regularly miss their co-workers. Most discover that it is important to replace these lost relationships quickly.

Chapter 6

Changing The Way
You Look At Work

Chapter 6

Changing The Way You Look At Work

"All work and no play makes Jack a dull boy—and Jill a rich widow."

Franklin P. Jones

Two Environments

You will notice that there is a circle within a circle in the perceptual field illustrated below. This is to remind us that we deal with two environments, work and personal, and that each influences the other.

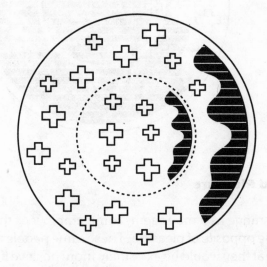

Let us assume the above illustration represents the focus on life of Alice, who makes a successful effort to concentrate on the positives in both environments and, as a result, enjoys working.

Now let us take Bob, whom we will assume has the same job and working environment as Alice. The only difference is that Bob is less successful in concentrating on positives. As a result, there is a dark cloud over most of the inner circle (work environment) and unfortunately it has spilled over into the outer circle (lifestyle).

ONE ENVIRONMENT INFLUENCES THE OTHER

Work and Pleasure

Strange as it may seem, some employees think of working as the opposite of pleasure. These same people mistakenly believe that they would be extremely more positive if they did not have to work. In other words, their unhappiness is based upon the way they *look at work*, not the work itself. In almost any other job they would have the same negative outlook.

Mark wants to be an upbeat person, but he has become increasingly negative about his job. The negatives—a difficult boss, work overload, and disagreeable clients—have swept the positive factors—good pay, excellent benefits, compatible co-workers—into the background. The result is that he has become more negative on the job and more difficult to deal with at home. In short, the attitude created by the way he sees his job is showing up in other areas of his life. Like many, Mark is not sufficiently disciplined to leave his negative attitude at work when he leaves for home.

A year ago, when Lois first joined the office staff, she would have rated her attitude as 90 percent positive. Today, she admits her outlook is often more negative than positive. She sometimes questions why she took the job in the first place. During her annual appraisal, her supervisor said: "You seem to have fallen into a trap. Instead of feeling good about work, you act as if what you do is just a job. Perhaps you have been listening too much to some negative co-workers. Unless you can restore the upbeat focus you had a year ago, you are playing a losing game."

What conclusions might you draw from these two cases? Here are a few possibilities:

- Any job can be more enjoyable by concentrating on the positives that are available in any work environment.

- Many employees do not realize they have almost the same control over negatives on the jobs as those found in their personal lives.

- It is impossible to keep negatives generated at work from spilling into one's personal life.

- Career success is ultimately dependent upon how one controls her or his attitude.

- Just as people often need a new focus in their lives, employees need a new focus on their jobs.

Negative Drift in the Work Environment

Some researchers believe that negative factors in work environments are on the rise. Studies indicate that job stress is a more powerful factor today than in the past. Additional pressure often comes from operating equipment such as computers where individual productivity is easily measured. Co-worker relationships in certain occupations can produce increased conflict because competition for jobs is more intense. Work tempos are accelerating. On top of all this, mergers, downsizing and corporate and government restructuring to make organizations "lean and mean" create insecurity. So do changes in ownership.

What does it mean? Simply that much work is not as relaxing and comfortable as it once was. This opens the door to negative drift. From another perspective, it means that during difficult times, it is more important than ever to maintain a positive workplace attitude—not just to keep management happy, not because greater productivity is required, *but because it is the best way to be upbeat in both the work and personal environments, and to satisfy yourself.*

In work situations, greater control of one's positive perceptual field can reverse things. At first, this may seem an impossible challenge because most employees tend to feel they have only minimum control over their work. Many tasks are inherently repetitive and boring. Still, it is always possible to make a "game" out of any assignment.

> *Norman is a garment cutter. It is his job to follow a design carefully as he cuts through many fabric layers at one time. How does he relieve the strain? Norman often imagines he is cutting a suit for the prime minister. His goal is to be so exact that newscasters will comment on how well dressed the prime minister is.*
>
> *Helen makes a game out of operating her word processor. She imagines she is in competition with her co-workers. Each time she improves her performance she declares herself a winner and gives herself a short break. Helen claims it makes her work more enjoyable and increases her productivity.*

The solution for these employees is not in changing their jobs but in the *way they look at their jobs.* In other words, employees who become negative and less effective must learn to see what creates this negativity and what they need to do to perform differently. They must use their minds to convert work into something positive. Easy to recommend. Easy to suggest. But how can it be accomplished?

How to Take a Look at Your Job

Let us assume that negative factors in your job are having a detrimental impact on your attitude and your life in general. You are aware of this and you do not like it. You decide to take remedial action. Your goal is to enjoy your job more, improve your career opportunities, and keep downbeat work factors from influencing your personal life. Following are four suggestions that will help you create a more positive focus on your specific job and in your lifestyle.

Suggestion 1:
Concentrate on your positive job factors. Your boss is naturally interested in your attitude because of the correlation between

productivity and the way a person is perceived by co-workers. Some organizations do a better job than others in providing a work environment that is conducive to positive attitudes. However, any organization can go only so far. In the final analysis, each person is ultimately responsible for his or her attitude. Reviewing personnel policies, forming teams, increasing pay and/or benefits can contribute, but even the best organization in the world cannot *make* you have a positive attitude.

Adel's Self-Appraisal

Adel is a registered nurse with leadership potential. She loves her lifestyle as a single woman, but she feels her career is losing promise. Adel admits that her negative attitude has been showing around the hospital recently. In talking it over with a friend who is a nursing superintendent at another hospital, the friend said: "You can wait around for management to do more than they are currently doing, until it is time to retire. Your hospital is as good or better than ours. If things improve on the job, it will come almost 100 percent from you and not from improvements made by management."

Last weekend, Adel listed everything negative about her job in one column and everything positive in the other. Next, she circled those negative factors to which she had given excessive mind-time. She made a vow to concentrate more on positive items over which she had control. In short, she would **talk, act and think about the positive factors.** *To help her do this, she posted the positive aspects of her job on the refrigerator. Within thirty days, Adel could sense her career was once again headed in the right direction and her life had become more fulfilling. Through mental discipline, blocking out the negatives and concentrating on the positives, she had defeated the negative drift that was keep-*

> ing her mind off of the positive factors that were present
> all along.

The bottom line is that you can control your attitude on the job in the same manner as in your personal life. *The same principles and techniques apply.*

When individuals have a persistently negative attitude toward work, they are doing both their employers and themselves a disservice. They should either seek another job or career, or do something to reverse their negative attitude. The first step in this process is to make a personal commitment to build a reputation as a professional worker, a person *who is a pleasure to be around.* The second step is to perceive the positive ahead of the negative and *show it in your behavior.* Keep in mind, none of this can happen unless you really want it to.

Suggestion 2:

View your job as a place you want to visit. To jazz up your life, you need to jazz up your attitude toward work. This means you need to take a more serendipitous approach—the way you look forward to a party. Try for a light-hearted, good-natured mood. One that will cause you to joke and have fun. *In other words, you should try to think of work as a place where many good things happen.*

> In recent months, Chad has been looking forward to Friday before he even arrived for work on Monday. Yesterday, his supervisor took him aside and said: "Chad, I'm going to give you a special assignment. As you know, I have been doing my best to get our staff to work together. My success has been moderate. I want you to play the role of an upbeat leader. I think you, more than anyone else on the staff, can do it. I have noticed that when you are working hard, but having fun, you create followers. All it will take is a little more leadership and your regular positive attitude.

What do you say?" Chad said yes to the suggestion and agreed to give it his best shot. Two weeks later there was more "team" spirit around and Chad was the talk of the department.

Consider approaching work in a lighter, more congenial and humorous mood. Think of it like driving a convertible with the top down on an open road on a summer day. Everything is invigorating. Ask yourself this question: *Why save all the happy times for the end of the workday?*

There is nothing in your job description that says you cannot have a good time while working. For example, what is wrong with getting your boss to laugh with you? Or having a fun relationship with a client? Or getting an invitation to lunch from a previously uncooperative co-worker? Or having a little craziness after a highly productive day?

Obviously, one should not expect a relaxed attitude over an eight-hour period. But few managers object to fun—especially when some levity can help mold a group into a more productive and efficient team.

Sherri observed that during the restructuring of her firm the attitudes of co-workers took a nosedive. Not wanting to fall into the same trap, she devised what she calls her 80/20 formula. In explaining it to a friend she said: "It's simple, I work 80 percent for the company and 20 percent for myself. I have picked up my productivity, but I am also squeezing in more time to have some fun on the job—not only during official breaks and lunchtime, but also in staff meetings and casual contacts. My personal attitude is much better and I think I am contributing to the team spirit my boss is always talking about. It's the only way I could figure how to up my own attitude and help others to. I recommend it!"

Every workplace *needs* people with happy, light-hearted attitudes, who can still produce at high levels and encourage others
to do the same. In fact, management both notices and rewards
these individuals.

- Janice, a top producer, simply walks away from co-workers
  who engage in negative talk. She shows up later with an
  upbeat or humorous comment that provokes laughter.

- Roy has the reputation with upper management as a professional on the move. This does not keep him from showing
  up with cookies from time to time or acting like a clown at
  the end of the day.

- Maisie, a supervisor for a telephone company, has a way of
  laughing at her job to release tensions. Some days, to set an
  upbeat tempo in her section, she deliberately dresses in an
  offbeat manner.

- Peter, a flight attendant, makes a game of his job by combin-
  ing excellent service with a little frivolity. When a flight is over,
  he receives many compliments.

- Gabriella, a computer operator, gets her attitude back on track
  now and then by doing mysterious little things like leaving
  crazy gifts around the office.

Work should not be a 40-hour weekly penalty. It should not
be something to *endure*. Rather, it should be a place where people feel good about themselves and their performance—a place
where their positive attitudes find expression.

Suggestion 3:
Permit a team approach to improve your attitude. When three
people are pushing a rock in opposite directions, the rock will
not budge. When the same people push in the same direction,
the rock will move. Wherever you work, whatever you do, be
a team member and cooperate with others to reach a common
goal. It is okay to do this for selfish reasons. Too often, when
we look at the team approach to productivity, we think of what
we can do for the team, *not what the team can do for us.*

When we participate in the work environment as a team member, we gain personally in many ways.

- We enjoy a feeling of acceptance that is not otherwise possible. Our peers give us recognition when we do well. There is a sense of "belonging," instead of isolation.

- We have the joy of participating in a common victory. We share in rewards along with others who also made it possible.

- We wind up with more friends, many of whom we can enjoy off the job.

Despite the rewards from team membership, many employees prefer to go it more alone. Carl is a good example.

Carl is an outstanding volleyball player. More than most team members, he is very generous in setting the ball up for others to kill. Everybody loves to play with Carl and he is often chosen as the team leader. At work, it is a different story. Carl prefers to work alone and seldom goes out of his way to help others.

Why is it that Carl does not see the connection? Is it because he has a mind-set that work is work and cannot be converted into a productivity game? Now, of course, playing volleyball is more pure fun than working—no argument there. But is the difference between the two less than Carl suspects? Would Carl have a more positive perspective at home if he used the team approach at work?

Suggestion 4:
Give yourself two promotions. If you can improve your attitude toward work, you will automatically give yourself two promotions. First, you will position yourself for future career moves that will mean you take home more money and better benefits.

Second, with a more positive attitude at work you will also discover you "take home" a better attitude.

Cary had his career on track for over three years. During this period, he viewed work as a competitive game and often stayed beyond normal working hours. Cary found the workplace fun, exciting, rewarding. His productivity was high. Life away from work was fulfilling.

Then, without being aware it was taking place, Cary started to complain about work. He began leaving work early. His girlfriend, Shirley, noticed the difference and mentioned it. Cary responded: "I'm just going through a down period. It doesn't amount to anything."

Weeks later, Cary said to Shirley: "I'm not sure I am cut out for work in the traditional sense. I think I'll quit my job and take some time off until I can find where I belong in life." Shirley said: "I don't think it is your job, I think it is your attitude. You've let the negative side of your job get to you. You are no fun anymore. You've lost your perspective and your charm and ambition along with it."

The following week Cary had a long talk with himself. What had gone wrong? Could he do an attitude turnaround? Could he force himself to seek all the good things that were still part of his life, including Shirley? On impulse, he called her and she agreed to meet him at their favorite place.

During the conversation, Cary said he was thinking about giving his job another six months with an upbeat, positive attitude, to see if he could get back his career perspective and enthusiasm. Shirley was delighted and said she would encourage and support him all the way.

Did it work? Six months later Shirley and Cary met at the same location to celebrate his new promotion.

As previously suggested, to permit a job to skew your perceptual field toward the negative is to defeat the very purpose of work. The compensation—salary and benefits—derived from work are supposed to keep financial problems—often a negative factor—to a minimum. Beyond that, work should be a positive experience in *itself*.

Work should not be the price you pay to support a good lifestyle—it should be a positive experience that contributes to one's total perceptual field.

Many people move from one job to another. Unfortunately many also carry their negative attitudes with them. Usually they are not aware they are doing this. Even though they give themselves the opportunity for a fresh start, they still wind up focusing on the negative side a few months after they change jobs. These individuals prove that it is not always job factors but inside perspective that is at fault.

Who Wants To Be a Triple Loser?

If you intend to put the suggestions contained in this chapter to work, you must first admit that permitting your job to turn you negative makes you a triple loser.

1. You enjoy your work less.

2. Your career progress is sidetracked.

3. Your personal life suffers.

Some jobs are better than others. Some work environments are better than others. But regardless of where you find yourself in the workplace today and tomorrow, only you can create the following perceptual field for yourself.

Chapter 7

Happy Talk

Happy Talk

> *"Good communication is as stimulating as black coffee, and just as hard to sleep after."*
>
> *Anne Morrow Lindbergh*

What you read in this chapter has not been scientifically verified. No research has been involved. Listening and observing on a casual basis provide the ideas presented. For example, you have probably observed that some of your family members, friends or co-workers either over-talk or say very little. You probably also noticed that the conversational theme of these same individuals tend to be either negative or positive, and what they say reflects their general attitude.

Do you also suspect that some over-talkers are more apt to dwell on negatives? *Might this mean these people learn to talk themselves into negative attitudes?*

Consider a man who was a delight to know until a few years away from retirement. At that time he was replaced by a younger person and given a less responsible role; he started to talk about the injustice of it all and he never stopped. Even after retirement he still inserted the situation into every possible conversation. It was like a cancer eating away at his perspective. In the end, he tainted what was an excellent career, lost the respect of co-workers, and chased friends away with his negative attitude induced by incessant negative talk.

Rod and Eva, in their late thirties with two children, feel fortunate to have their parents within easy visiting distance.

> There is, however, a serious problem. A visit to Eva's parents is a fun trip for all. Conversations provide encouragement. On the other hand, a visit to Rod's parents is a downer. Rod comments: "My folks seem to have everything, but their casual conversations are so negative we always leave in a bad mood. All of their talk centers around what is wrong. I guess they have chased their friends away so they unload on us. Our teenagers love to visit Eva's folks. They beg to stay home when we go to see mine. We'd like to spread our visiting time equally but we don't do it anymore."

The conclusion may be that some people fall into a trap of their own making. Those that gripe talk more and enjoy it less, while others with a positive "talk discipline" say less but enjoy it more. A perceptual field illustration might picture it this way.

Definition of a Happy or Positive Talker

A "Happy Talker" is a conversationalist who introduces and deals primarily with upbeat subjects. This does not mean she or he refuses to take a strong position or challenge others. It simply means that the individual refuses to bore others with personal complaints, unnecessary criticism or whining. "Happy Talkers" love and support intriguing conversations that are intellectually stimulating. They also often play the devil's advocate. They enjoy injecting humor into communications. They feel strongly that everyone involved should have equal time. They realize that verbal communication is a projection of their attitudes.

For some reason, incessant talkers often seem to view the negative side of living more than the positive. These individuals feel the need to relate their views to others. It is generally recognized as good therapy to "talk unfortunate incidents and frustrations out of your system." At times, we all have the need to do this. We feel better by "letting off steam" through the safety-valve of talking. But satisfying this need does not explain why over-talkers consistently dwell on the negative.

Are these talkers falling victim to their own over-talking habits? Is the media responsible? Do they enjoy negative talk to focus on their own, more fortunate status? Or is their negative talk a giveaway to the fact that their focus has turned negative and they refuse to do anything about it?

Understanding the Advantages of Talk Discipline

Just as we have the power to concentrate mentally on positive factors, we also have the power to keep our conversations with others on a positive track. It takes discipline. But many people seem to have what it takes.

Gerald lives with a simple credo he learned from his mother: "If you can't say something good about another person, don't say anything." Gerald has taken this policy and translated it into a more comprehensive idea: "If you can't say something positive about life, don't say anything except in the decision-making process when you are satisfied you have the facts on your side." Gerald is an excellent example of a most successful manager who has mastered the skill of talk-discipline.

Jenny refuses to "bad mouth" others and is successful, like Gerald, in keeping her comments on the positive side. But she goes one step further by intervening in some conversations in an attempt to get topics back on a positive track. For example, at work, when a co-worker is talking negatively about working conditions or management, Jenny might delicately interrupt and say "I think we are going

---

> *through a big change and the more we do to help, the more secure our jobs will be. I want our company to be a survivor. Don't you?"*

People who continually introduce negative topics of little consequence in their conversations, such as constant complaining, seem to ignore the premise that you need to "talk" positive to *be* positive. They ignore even the possibility of a connection between the act of talking and mental focus. As a consequence, they lose friends and convert themselves into a more negative frame of mind.

HAPPY TALK EXERCISE

Based upon the ideas expressed so far, complete the following exercise. If you feel the statement is true, circle the T; if you feel it is false, circle the F.

T   F   Funny storytellers have, on the average, more positive perspectives than non-funny storytellers.

T   F   Those who adhere to the policy "if you can't say something good about someone, don't say anything," usually have more positive attitudes than others.

T   F   When a problem is involved, talking about it can be therapeutic to the talker.

T   F   Excessive talkers often seem more negative than others.

T   F   Happy conversations translate into positive thoughts; positive thoughts translate into happy conversations; both translate into more positive attitudes.

T   F   Positive people deliberately feed their minds positive thoughts.

T   F   The more you complain about your situation, the more negative your general attitude becomes.

T   F   People who, through uplifting conversations, help others remain positive also help their own attitudes.

T   F   It is easier to talk yourself into a negative mood than to talk yourself out of one.

T   F   It is easier to think yourself into a negative mood than to think or talk yourself out of one.

AUTHOR'S NOTE: In the opinion of the author, all of the above statements are true. The purpose of the exercise is to communicate the importance of *what we talk about* to the state of our perceptual fields. Positive talk normally gives us a more positive focus on life.

Telling Jokes Can Be Viewed as Self-Serving Attitude Boosters

To satisfy curiosity, several individuals were asked why they tell funny stories.

Three answers surfaced. These include:

1. Telling jokes and funny stories are ways to gain attention and recognition. Clever and sensitive joke-tellers are often more popular than those who prefer to listen.

2. The process of telling jokes helps both the teller and the receiver. Depending upon the skill of the teller, and the story, it can be a positive, relaxing experience for everyone.

3. Consciously or unconsciously, people often remember and tell jokes to keep their attitudes more positive. In short, they cheer themselves up.

Following were some interesting comments from people who regularly tell what they hope will be funny stories:

"I tell jokes more for myself than for others, but I am selective. Doom and gloomers are seldom amused and unless people really laugh, it is not worth the effort."

"When I was a manager, I always received better productivity from many employees when I told a few suitable stories to lift their spirits."

"When I am teaching, I always start out with jokes or stories that I enjoy telling and have not previously been circulated. In doing this, I gain more student support, but the big advantage is that I find myself relaxing and doing a better job."

Some joke-tellers *understand* that a primary purpose in telling stories is to improve their personal attitudes. In short, they are self-serving. Bravo! You cannot just wait around, hoping someone will give your attitude a boost.

Not All Complainers Have Something to Complain About

Have you noticed that some people who have a legitimate reason to complain, do less complaining than others? Do you, for example, know a person who is handicapped or has suffered a personal tragedy, yet is a more positive conversationalist than others who, in reality, have little to overcome?

When a medical doctor who has a patient who has fought off incurable cancer for over ten years was asked how this could be, he replied: "Elaine doesn't dwell on her problem by complaining or feeling sorry for herself. Rather, she goes around trying to make others feel better. At times she is so upbeat I feel ashamed of my attitude."

Nora is a practical nurse in a skilled nursing home where residents require 24-hour care. In asking whether or not she had favorite patients, she replied. "Absolutely. For example, I have one lady who is so grateful, pleasant and humorous that I can't help spending more time with her. If I am late helping her, she teases me in a delightful manner. If everyone else complains about the food, she'll joke about it. I can't help wanting to give her more attention, if for no other reason than to help my personal attitude. Positive people always get more attention whether in hospitals or care facilities."

Happy Talk as a Refocusing Mechanism

It may be stretching the "talk discipline" idea too far, but at times it seems that just talking in an upbeat vein may reinforce our positive mental focus. For example, looking back on the teaching profession, it seems that those who love their subjects always transmit positive images to students. They obviously spend hours talking about their subject in a positive way. Thus, these select teachers become positive people in the lives of others. From a different point of view, it might be fair to say that "if you want to be a positive person, select a subject you have a passion for, and then teach or share it with others."

Happy talk can be an attitude refocusing mechanism for some individuals. If so, they have found one of life's top secrets.

Test the Impact of a Negative Conversation on Your Positive Attitude

Do you remember an evening when you were with friends and the conversation became so involved and uplifting that you thought about it weeks later? Positive discussions, between two people or a small group, can lift everyone's attitude, especially when there is plenty of laughter and everyone has a chance to contribute.

On the other hand, a one-sided, negative conversation or discussion can be a real downer. You might not be able to sleep because you remain emotionally upset from too much negative conversation from one person. Often it takes time to get your attitude back into a positive focus.

Test the Impact of a Negative Conversation

If you would like to "test" how your attitude responds to negative vs positive conversations, you might try this experiment:

Situation #1:

Either alone or with a spouse or friend, arrange a visit with someone you have avoided because the communication usually turns negative. While the visit is taking place, give the person being visited freedom to talk about all sorts of problems. Do not attempt to sidetrack the individual or individuals into a more positive conversation track. Let the negative talk roll. The less laughter the better.

Situation #2:
For comparison, visit a second party with a reputation for being upbeat during conversations—*someone you like to visit*. Do your best to keep the conversation on a positive track. Confine your contributions to positive things only. The more laughter the better.

Once both visits are over, answer the following questions:

COMPARISON	Negative Talk		Positive Talk	
1. Did you want to extend the visit?	Yes	No	Yes	No
2. After the visitation, were you stimulated or depressed?	Yes	No	Yes	No
3. Were you more positive when you left than when you arrived?	Yes	No	Yes	No
4. Was your attitude in better focus as a result of the visit?	Yes	No	Yes	No
5. Do you wish to go back for a second visit soon?	Yes	No	Yes	No

In comparing the two situations, it is likely you gave more YES answers to the "positive talk" experience.

What else might you have learned from conducting such an experiment? Or from assuming you did one in your mind? Rather than provide possible answers, consider the following questions on page 82.

When people visit you, are their attitudes more positive when they leave? If so, what does this mean about you as a conversationalist?

Would such an experiment provide additional light on the value of having a "disciplined mind"?

Might such an experiment give support to the idea that "Happy Talk" can be viewed as an attitude refocusing mechanism?

How To Monitor Your Own Talking

The art of training yourself to become a disciplined and positive talker is a worthy endeavor, especially if you do so to improve your positive attitude. Here are a few tips to consider:

- Recognize that confining your casual conversations to upbeat topics is a major step toward becoming a more positive person.

- When you need to get a negative incident or problem out of your system, do it with a friend who recognizes your need and who would ask the same favor from you. Gloom and doom spreaders pay a high price in lost friendships and negative attitudes.

- If you like to challenge yourself, try to be a positive talker a majority of the time. Reserve the minority for serious discussions related to problem solving.

- Practice the skill of being a good subject converter—that is, learn how to move a casual or non-problem conversation from the negative to the positive for the benefit of your own attitude and that of others.

- Shorten the time you spend with incessantly negative talkers who refuse to switch to the positive. In some cases, sever the relationship.

- If telling jokes or stories comes naturally to you, continue the practice without overdoing it.

- Make a stronger, more concerted effort to be a model "talk discipline" person, even if you discover that you talk less.

The techniques of good communication—voice control, diction, etc.—are important. *What you say* in casual conversation is also important. The truth is that the more you value your positive attitude, the more significant "happy talk" becomes.

Chapter 8

"Play It Safe, Lena"

Play It Safe, Lena

"The first and great commandment is, Don't let them scare you."
Elmer Davis

Sometimes you need to reach age 60 or beyond before you can look back on your life to determine what basic mistakes may have been made. In writing *Comfort Zones: A Practical Guide For Retirement Planning*, I interviewed a great number of people who had the insightful perception that comes from living a long time. What was the number one mistake these people admitted to?

The answer is reflected in this quotation from an anonymous 85-year-old woman. The piece is entitled "Traveling Light" and can be found in other publications.

"If I had my life to live over, I'd dare to make more mistakes next time. I'd relax. I would limber up. I would be sillier than I have been this trip. I would take fewer things seriously. I would take more chances. I would take more trips. I would climb more mountains, swim more rivers. I would eat more ice cream and less beans. I would perhaps have more actual troubles but I would have fewer imaginary ones.

You see, I'm one of those people who live seriously and sanely hour by hour, day after day. Oh, I've had my moments, and if I had to do it over again, I'd have more of them. In fact, I'd try to have nothing else, just moments one after another, instead of living so many years ahead of each day. I've been one of those persons who never goes anywhere without a thermometer, a hot water bottle, a rain-

coat and a parachute. If I had it to do again, I would travel lighter than I have.

If I had to live my life over, I would start barefoot earlier in the spring and stay later in the fall. I would go to more dances. I would ride more merry-go-rounds. I would pick more daisies."

Most people who reflect on a long life wish they had taken more risks. Why didn't they? It narrows down to the fact that they permitted *natural doubts to cloud their positive perspectives.*

We all carry doubts around with us. Should I complete my education? Should I travel more? Should I remarry? Should I change my career? Hidden behind these doubts is a fear that things will not work out, so why take the chance? Why not be satisfied with the way things are? *Why not play it safe?*

Doubts Expand the Negative Side of Our Perceptual Fields

There is nothing wrong with caution or being conservative. But the truth is that most people play it too safe. In so doing, they lose their potential to be more positive.

A doubt is a distrust of your ability to make a right decision. It is an unsettling feeling that you might embarrass yourself or lose what you already possess. Or it can be a suspicion that things will not work out. *Doubts signal lack of confidence in the future.* A doubt is usually a negative in your perceptual field.

In the illustration below, you will notice that doubts are visualized in the form of question marks inside of hypothetical boxes. The idea is to portray doubts as significant negatives that are boxed or "locked into" our perceptual fields, where they are difficult to release and destroy.

PERCEPTUAL FIELD CLOUDED WITH DOUBTS

When Elisabeth was 28, circumstances forced her and her husband into personal bankruptcy. Although Elisabeth contributed a second income to family finances, neither she nor her husband could delay purchases. The result was that they were always deeply in debt. Their inability to manage money eventually caused a rift and they went their separate ways. Unfortunately, Elisabeth carried the bankruptcy stigma with her and from then on, her "doubts" on any decision involving money doubled. Result? She carried so many doubts that she was afraid to live. It was not until her second husband restored confidence in her that she was once again free.

Jay, now 58, had led a conservative life, primarily because he had permitted himself to be over-influenced by his wife, who had based decisions on whether or not it would be a "safe" move rather than whether it would be a rewarding one. Result? Jay had felt stifled and unfulfilled. Upon retirement, has was somehow able to convince his wife that it was now time to take some reasonable risks. Through

> both conversations and experiences they helped each
> other dissipate their doubts. Today, with more confidence
> and courage, retirement has turned into the best time
> in their lives.

Sources of Doubts

Doubts, and the fears upon which they are based, spring from
many sources. Early childhood experiences are responsible for
some, but adult experiences also contribute. A miscarriage can
create a cloud over having a full-term baby. The loss of a job
injects doubts about one's ability to compete. Rejection from a
special person will almost always be a "doubt creator." All such
experiences create negative "mind sets" that may last a lifetime
and do irreparable damage to a positive attitude.

What Happens When Doubts
are Removed?

Let us assume that you can identify three doubts that you suspect keep you from being the kind of person you want to be.
For example, you might be inclined toward one of the following
possibilities. You might: (1) fear going "broke," (2) be afraid of
losing a friend or (3) worry over a long-term health problem.
Chances are you will devote a great deal of "mind-time" to these
doubts. Frequently, even when everything else is positive in life,
you will probably permit these potential "dark clouds" to move
into your perceptual field. Chances are that you will worry excessively about them. Sometimes it will be impossible for you to
see the bright view beyond.

What would happen if you could wash doubts, similar to those
above, out of your perceptual field? Permit the following illustration on page 91 to tell the story.

PERCEPTUAL FIELD WITH FEW DOUBTS

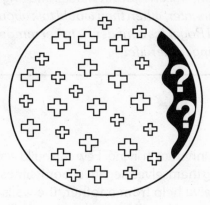

Like most people, given the choice, you would concentrate more on positives than negatives. The result is that your attitude would improve. Also, you would be able to slow any negative drift. But do not stop here. Would making such an improvement in the focus on your environment make it possible for a more enjoyable and fulfilling life?

Sean is so uncomfortable about his ability to dance that he avoids any social event that involves dancing. He also avoids giving a talk in front of a group. Consistent doubts in these directions have caused Sean to be over-cautious. At 33, he met Jean who loved to dance and had confidence in her speaking abilities. What happened? Together, Jean and Sean decided to take dancing lessons and a public speaking course. Today, Sean is a totally different, more confident person in all aspects of his life.

When Justine met Roger, she was so overweight that she doubted he would be attracted to her. Having tried a dozen times to lose weight and improve her image, she had given

> up. But Roger, with his upbeat attitude, did not go away.
> Soon, Justine found herself making new commitments.
> Years later, when they would talk about early times, Justine
> told Roger his confidence in her removed many doubts and
> changed her life.

Risk

Risk is inherent in living. Few can build walls of protection without turning themselves negative. Sometimes, when we are fortunate to receive help from another, the walls of doubt can be eliminated and life will become more exciting. At other times, getting rid of a few doubts is a do-it-yourself project. If you wish to discover the role doubts may be playing in your life, truthfully answer the following questions and *check your answers with comments from the author.* This exercise might help you eliminate, or at least downplay, some doubts you carry with you.

QUESTIONS ABOUT DOUBTS

Are unnecessary doubts keeping you from the upbeat attitude that is rightfully yours? To find out, please answer the following questions:

	YES	NO
1. Are you still having doubts about taking action in some area, because of an unfortunate experience in your past?	☐	☐
2. Do you need a new procedure to help you make better decisions faster?	☐	☐
3. Are you a person who worries excessively over negative possibilities that will probably never occur?	☐	☐
4. Do a few people call you a "worry wart"?	☐	☐
5. Do you agree that the consequences of making a poor decision are seldom as severe as you anticipate?	☐	☐
6. Do you agree that the removal of a single doubt or "hang-up" in your perceptual field would help you be more positive?	☐	☐
7. If you could get rid of one doubt, would it help you dispose of others?	☐	☐
8. Is it more difficult for you to make a decision today than it was five years ago?	☐	☐
9. Do you disagree with the idea that after living 50 full and rewarding years, taking risks should be easier because there is less to lose if you fail?	☐	☐
10. Are doubts about the future keeping your focus negative?	☐	☐

Interpreting Your Answers

To interpret your answers, please note the comments of the author below:

1. A yes answer indicates you are needlessly carrying around a negative factor in your perceptual field, because you were "snake bit" over something in the past. Is it time you forget or forgive so you are no longer a victim?

2. A yes answer indicates you could benefit from the kind of decision-making procedure you might find in a good management book. Go the library and ask for material on *How To Make Better Decisions.* Knowing *how* to make good decisions could dissipate some of the worry you have over the future.

3. A yes answer means that you have lost some of your confidence about the future. As a result, your attitude is more negative than it should be. Remember, the more good things you expect from the future, the more you will receive.

4. A worry-wart is a person who tends to worry needlessly about insignificant things. If you fall into this category, you are carrying some negative baggage around that is causing you to be more negative than otherwise would be the case.

5. A yes answer means you should be congratulated because you are saying that you can make a poor decision and probably live through it, without it dragging you down to a negative level. In short, you do not exaggerate the consequences of making a mistake to the point it turns you negative and you procrastinate.

6. Bravo, if you answered yes. Just because a first marriage did not work does not mean a second one will not. Just because you got seasick on one cruise does not mean you will on a second trip. The more "hang-ups" you hold, the more negative you will be.

7. Sure it would! Once an individual no longer doubts his or her ability to do something—dance, pilot a plane, etc.—it will give the person more confidence to do other things—- like learning to swim or losing weight.

8. A yes answer here indicates that you may be becoming more negative because you are postponing decisions and letting things worry you more than in the past and more than necessary. You cannot be positive unless you anticipate that good things will happen in your future.

9. Wonderful, providing you gave a yes answer. If a person has lived a rather long and fulfilling life, it should mean this person has less to lose—none of us live forever—so it should be easier to take risks. In the game of life, the longer you live the fewer chips—years—you have to play. With only a few chips left, why worry?

10. At this point, you are in a position to know how many doubts you have about the future and *how much impact they are having on your attitude.* A yes answer means it is time for you to do something about it. Please remember, life is an attitude and you can see what you want to see in your future.

Lena: A Case Study

It is said that doubts increase and become more of a handicap the older one becomes. Lena demonstrated that this need not be the case.

> *Lena was trained by her conservative parents to always play it safe. As a result, she turned down some promising relationships. She also refused to leave the security of her first job for a more dynamic career. At age 40, she came to the realization that life was passing her by. Then, a stroke of good luck changed her life. To help a charitable cause, Lena*

purchased a raffle ticket and won a free vacation to Hawaii for two. Doubting that it would be in her comfort zone, she thought of giving the tickets away when, talking to a cousin in Tennessee by telephone, the cousin replied: "Gee! I'd love to go with you. We'd have a ball!" Not having seen the cousin for years, Lena was still doubtful, but with an untypical spark of confidence she called back and said: "Let's do it!"

Everything about the trip fell into place gracefully. Under the wing of her more assertive cousin, Lena gained additional confidence each day. On the flight home they decided to take a second trip to Mexico the following spring. But something much deeper and significant occurred inside Lena. For the first time in her life, she found herself accepting social invitations without hesitation. Before spring arrived, she had joined a health club, completed a course in dancing, learned to swim, and earned a substantial career promotion. Lena had erased many doubts from her perceptual field and her more positive attitude mirrored the loss. The second trip was more fun than the first.

Chapter 9

"Get It Done, Roger"

Chapter 9

Get It Done, Roger

Positive people are far more likely than others to face up to problems, make tough decisions and refuse to look back. This is how they maintain their personal productivity. This is how they act when trouble strikes. Positive people do not ignore problems. They handle them with dispatch.

It is easy to get the mistaken impression that those with an optimistic attitude are simply happy-go-lucky people that fate allows to float, unperturbed, on cloud nine. Not so! Positive people often have more problems, because they take more risks. What distinguishes them is their refusal to let problems continue to nag away at them. Rather, they jump in quickly, address the problems and get on with life. If there are consequences, they accept them and keep moving forward. They realize that staying positive is more important than any temporary setback they encounter.

John, a highly successful sales representative, was called in for a tax audit. Knowing that he had been sloppy in his record-keeping and that he may have charged off more on his home office space than allowed, a dark cloud formed over his mental focus as he worried excessively instead of getting ready. He neglected his job and his sales commissions plunged. He applied for and received a delay on the audit. Final result? John paid two penalties instead of one. The most damaging was to his attitude.

Grace was 29 when she received her divorce and started a new life with a new car, new wardrobe and new attitude. The only problem was that she financed her new life with excessive credit card purchases. When the squeeze came, she faced a sobering challenge. Although she worried and devoted much mind-time to her problem, she reacted slowly and refused to face the full scope of the problem. As a result, it took her four years to dig herself out of the hole. Grace's attitude became so negative during the recovery period that she was passed over for two promotions. Looking back, Grace admits that she paid three times as much for her purchases as was necessary — one ticket price and double that on what eventually happened to her attitude.

Vince knew he might be delaying the inevitable by not paying his parking tickets, but he procrastinated until the police impounded his car and presented him with a bill so high that he had to borrow money to recover it. Although he shrugged the problem off as just "one of those things," he eventually discovered that the real price he paid was in a more negative attitude. "I didn't accept the fact that I was carrying a big negative around with me for all those months. I just thought I was being smart when, in fact, I was victimizing myself with a negative attitude."

People who truly appreciate the power of a positive attitude do not allow problems to accumulate and expand. They act quickly and decisively in solving problems so that negatives are eliminated and the positive factors in their lives take over again.

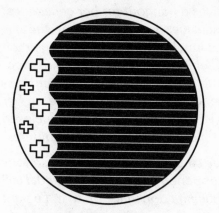 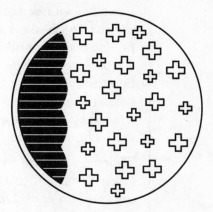

Perceptual field of people who allow problems to accumulate.   **Perceptual field of those who deal with problems quickly.**

Unsolved Problems Invite Negative Attitudes

It is a tough lesson to learn, but allowing problems to remain unsolved invites disaster. Most problems become bigger and bigger. And once these problems burst, the attitude damage has been so severe that recovery is slow and demanding. How can such situations be avoided? Here are three suggestions:

Suggestion 1:

Face up to the problem. Most of us have ways of deceiving ourselves about problems, which is why we fail to recognize that just carrying problems around in our subconscious minds can hurt our attitude.

Until we admit we have a problem and start to do something about it, the clouds just get heavier.

Elaine admitted she enjoyed the life of a scrambler. She moved from one firm to another, always accepting more responsibility and earning a higher salary. She found herself so involved in her career that there was little time left over. For example, Elaine usually spent time after work in a cocktail lounge that was a hangout for her colleagues, discussing job-related activities over drinks. Soon she was having a drink or two at lunch. Then, one evening when she was working late, Elaine's boss dropped by and mentioned how drinking could negatively influence career success. The next day she found a sealed envelope on her desk. A booklet on the dangers of alcoholism was enclosed with a note that read, "Here's to your positive attitude."

That night, Elaine drove straight home and had a serious talk with herself. "It's happened. I'm getting hooked. I will lose my career and my life if I don't face up to it. I've got to get on the wagon by myself now or face professional help later. Can I do it? Sure I can."

And she did! A year later, when she was appointed to the role of vice president, her ex-boss made the presentation with a twinkle in her eye.

Suggestion 2:
Make tough decisions. It is said that many excellent managers who desire to become leaders never make it, because they have not trained themselves to make tough decisions. Many managers are able to get the important facts, involve others, and come up with options. Only a few know how to bite the bullet and make the final decision with clarity and decisiveness.

Making tough decisions may be even more difficult in our personal lives than in business.

When it came to playing golf, Gary had three psychological things going against him. He was over-competitive and frequently lost his temper over a weak shot or missed putt. He had a passion for gambling and often doubled his bet when losing a hole. Gary also had the potential to be an outstanding golfer, and he knew it. As a result, he would often start out with his favorite foursome in a positive way, but before the game was over he would be totally negative.

One afternoon, almost a year ago, Gary got so frustrated with himself that he decided to take some golf lessons. But every time he got ready to sign up, he backed away. Finally, he stopped by a driving range where no one knew him, found a pro who agreed to work with him, and signed up. At the end of the second lesson, the pro turned into a counselor and told Gary: "You have a great swing and you know the techniques of golf, but you have a lousy attitude toward the game. Every hole is a life or death matter with you. Every bad shot you make causes you to lose your rhythm. Until you learn to smile instead of scream at a simple mistake, I can't help you."

Gary got the message and regained his focus on the game as a pleasure activity, not a matter of life or death. Everyone in his foursome complimented him on his change in attitude and how much better his game had become.

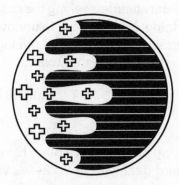

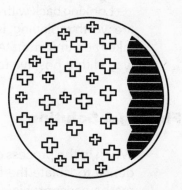

Perceptual field of people who oscillate making decisive decisions.

Perceptual field of those who make tough decisions and accept consequences.

Suggestion 3:

Never look back. Most of us do some crying over spilled milk. We look back and replay our mistakes over and over in our minds. We ask ourselves unanswerable questions. Why did I do this or that? Usually the only thing we accomplish in doing this is to cloud our focus on life and make ourselves more negative.

Mr. and Mrs. Taylor sold their lovely home and moved into a less expensive townhouse. It was just before the big increase in prices took place. Now they constantly look back and talk about how much money they lost by selling when they did. Their negative attitudes have chased their friends away and helped to ruin what could have been a happy retirement.

In contrast to Mr. and Mrs. Taylor, the Greenwalds, under similar circumstances, joke about their lousy timing. They understand that things have a way of balancing out and do not dwell on what occurred.

Looking back with an upbeat attitude, seeking the events that are worth replaying, is one thing; looking back to uncover mistakes and unfortunate circumstances is another. Looking either way with a positive focus is the formula that works.

Finding A Solution

When in the process of solving problems, we often have a tendency to isolate the facts and deal with them as we would a mathematics problem, looking for a "right" answer. Most of life's problems are more complex. Other factors are involved. How does one solution influence others? Will the solution simplify my life or make it more complicated? Will I victimize myself if I attempt to help others? And, most important of all, what will happen to my personal attitude? *Will the solution make me more positive or negative?*

Which Comes First?
Attitude or the Solution?

The old teaser "which comes first, the chicken or the egg?" comes into play when thinking of how important our attitudes are in decision-making.

Most of us make a major mistake if we do not connect our attitude to the solution of a problem. For example, we should stay away from making big decisions when we are negative and depressed. Why? Because we are not in focus. In the midst of a bad mood, it is likely that we will not see problems clearly. As a result, we often compound the problem with a poor decision. Wise people learn to postpone important decisions, for a few hours or a few days, until the decision-making mood strikes. Only when in a positive frame of mind should problems be faced squarely. This will lead to the best decisions.

How much value do you place on a positive attitude? Do you consider it to be almost as valuable as life itself? If so, you will probably accept the challenge of facing up to problems, making difficult decisions, living with them with class, *and quickly bouncing back with the same positive attitude you had at the beginning.*

It is a giant challenge but the smart thing to do!

Positive People Protect Their Attitudes
By Always Having a Plan B

A Plan B is simply an optional alternative, should your preferred Plan A fall apart. It is being *ready and prepared* to take a different route if it becomes necessary or advisable. A Plan B is, in effect, an insurance policy that you hope you will not need to use.

Assume for a moment that Alice and Bob are happy working for an organization that is in the process of downsizing. Both recognize that their jobs could be eliminated. Alice is most insecure about the possibility of losing her job. She complains about it all the time, *but does nothing.* Bob, on the other hand, senses the reality of the situation and develops a Plan B for himself. His plan involves updating his resume, taking a refresher course on his specialty, arranging for interviews with other organizations through a networking system he has maintained, and saying to himself: "I like my job here, but I am ready and willing to make a move if my job is eliminated. My Plan B is preparing me to find a better job elsewhere. The more I work on my Plan B, the more confident I become."

Who is doing the best job in protecting their positive attitude? Obviously, it is Bob, because he is not waiting around feeling insecure, but taking action to prepare for a possible change. Not only will he have a more positive attitude working under his Plan A, in his current job, but he will be more competitive in the labor market with a Plan B under his arm.

Despite the advantages of having a job Plan B, few people develop one. Or, if they do, it is primarily in their heads and little action is involved. Many worry a lot. Some relax while receivng unemployment insurance payments. Others refuse to explore the employment market with a good plan and a positive perspective.

How a Plan B Helps to Keep One Positive

Research has shown that having a good Plan B not only helps people should they lose their jobs, it almost always makes them happier in their present jobs, Plan A.

When Melinda's firm announced a reorganization plan, she was aware of her lack of seniority. She realized that her job might be eliminated. Quickly, Melinda started to put

> together a Plan B—spending much of her spare time on
> the project. While the attitudes of her co-workers, without
> Plan B's, became increasingly negative, Melinda started
> to see the possibilities of a better future for herself elsewhere.
> Result? She started improving her skills on her present job
> and learning everything possible that might help her win
> another. This enabled her to maintain a more positive atti-
> tude, increase her personal productivity, and eventually
> Melinda's Plan B got her a better job in the same organi-
> zation.

The Plan B Concept Works in Many Situations

As a writer, I have always tried to work on more than one project
at the same time. This helps me from feeling negative when I
receive a rejection notice. It is the "don't put all of your eggs in
one basket" approach that works best for me. Having a Plan B
can be a smart move in many other areas:

- When planning a vacation, it is a good idea to have a second
  option, in case travel accommmodations or other factors force
  a change in plans.

- High school graduates are encouraged to apply to several col-
  leges, so if their first choice does not work out, they have a
  Plan B in place.

- When taking someone out to dinner, your first choice of a
  restaurant might be so crowded there could be a long wait.
  A second choice, already in your mind, could give you an
  even better evening.

- When selling a home, it is good insurance to have two plans
  ready. One, in the event your home sells quickly, and you
  have no place to stay until your new home is ready and a
  second plan, in the event it takes many months to sell.

Good planners always have a Plan B that can be put into operation immediately. Although these individuals may not say their second choice is a *way to keep a positive attitude*, it usually turns out that way.

> *Dan's job was to set up franchises for a specialty product within certain geographical areas. Only one franchisee could be selected. In doing his research, Dan always tried to find the best outlet for his product, and he always had a Plan B. His strategy was to offer his Plan A the opportunity, but if things did not work out, he would immediately go to his Plan B with the same enthusiasm he had when he approached Plan A. Often, he discovered, the Plan B outlet turned out to be the best. The important thing was that, by having two options, Dan kept his attitude from turning negative.*

Fire, health and accident insurance policies are designed to protect us from unforeseen financial disasters. Plan B's, and sometimes C's and D's, are designed to protect us from unexpected attitude adjustments. One can be as important as the other.

PLAN A ONLY   **PLAN A & B**

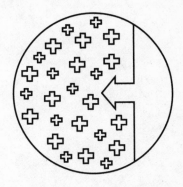

Perceptual field of
people who look back
and focus on mistakes.

Perceptual field of those
who look back and
focus on positives.

Chapter 10

Incoming Negatives

Chapter 10

Incoming Negatives

> *"If the grass is greener in the other fellow's yard—let him worry about cutting it."*
>
> *Fred Allen*

So far, we have been discussing how to expand current positives and diminish negatives. These are factors that exist now. *They are already in your perceptual field.* What about positives and negatives that will enter your focus in the future? How will you deal with them?

As far as positives are concerned, we can yell horray and enjoy them as they come. The more the better. Those that come your way should be appreciated and coveted. Every so often, we should reflect on the good aspects of our lives—our health, friends and family. As we have learned, the more positives we anticipate, the more we are apt to receive. Whatever you take with you into the next decade, be sure to include a serendipitous attitude.

But what about negatives? Here we have a problem that cries for attention. What can we do to minimize *unexpected* negatives? Advance understanding and preparation is part of the answer.

Minor Jolts and Major Blows

In boxing, professionals learn to take jolts on the chin and keep fighting. But all boxers live in fear that a major blow will knock them out and possibly end their careers. The negatives of life that enter into our perceptual fields can be classified in the same way.

A Minor Jolt

Minor jolts—little pieces of bad news that seem to hit us on a weekly basis—deserve one kind of treatment.

> *It was a negative week for Sally. She got off to a bad start, because of a dead battery Monday morning. It took until Thursday for her to get back into focus.*

A Major Blow

Major blows—those that happen infrequently, but that may take a year or more to live through—require another approach.

> *The telephone call came late at night. Jessica's mother, in her early fifties, had died from complications following routine surgery.*

Minor jolts often upset us emotionally, but the damage is usually temporary. Major blows, on the other hand, can knock us, and our attitudes, down for a long count.

Minor Jolts Can Accumulate and Turn You Negative

Most people can endure single jolts without losing focus. When a series of jolts hits however, more time is needed to regain a positive perspective.

Kayli would like to forget the summer of 1991. After taking a delightful one week vacation, she discovered she had some unexpected bills to pay that would keep her grounded for at least three months. Then, her roommate moved unexpectedly, causing even more financial strain. On top of that, Kayli fell and in addition to wearing a cast on her wrist for three weeks, she also had to pay doctor bills. Then, when the summer was almost over, she received the bad news that her car needed major repair.

Kayli could have handled a single minor negative in her stride, but the accumulation put her attitude into a blue funk. It was almost Christmas before she was back on track.

Recovery Techniques That May Fit Your Comfort Zone

None of us is exempt from receiving frequent minor jolts. There is no way to keep all of them out of our focus. The question is, how can we learn to roll with punches that slip through our defenses?

Here are some techniques that will help you dispense with most incoming negatives in a graceful manner, so that even your closest friends will not know you have been engaged in some "inside refocusing."

HOW TO KEEP MINOR JOLTS FROM IMPACTING YOUR ATTITUDE

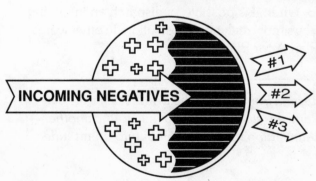

INCOMING NEGATIVES

#1 Filter some out of your mind through immediate action.

#2 When appropriate, erase the negative by switching to a Plan B.

#3 If possible, convert the negative into a positive.

Technique 1:

Filter the jolt out of your perceptual field immediately—before it consumes some of your valuable mind time. The moment it hits, take care of it! For example, if you receive an unexpected bill and you have money in the bank to cover it, write a check immediately. Do not let it bug you for several days before you write a check. Take your loss and get it over with so you do not have to pay two prices—both the money and a negative attitude.

Or, let us assume you react emotionally to a certain situation and in the process hurt your relationship with a close friend or co-worker. What should you do? Apologize immediately so that the incident does not clutter your perceptual field with another negative. Restore the relationship, and even more important, keep it from hanging around and doing damage to your attitude.

> *A few moments after Steven lost his cool, he knew he had damaged his relationship with Ashlee. After losing sleep and feeling edgy for more than a week, Steven apologized and started to rebuild the relationship. When things got back to normal, he realized he had needlessly gone through an emotional merry-go-round. He said to himself: "Next time, I will act immediately."*

Technique 2:

Switch to Plan B. Often it is possible to dispatch an incoming negative quickly, by simply making a substitution. In other words, abandon your Plan A for Plan B.

> *When A.J. returned from a trip to the South Pacific, he discovered that Jane, his steady girlfriend, had found another guy. Rather than letting the "hurt" grow into an attitude*

> *problem, A.J. called Michelle, another friend, and invited her to dinner.*
>
> *For some time, Brad had been thinking about moving into an apartment of his own. When he heard that his job would be eliminated and the only way he could stay with his firm would be to move to another location, he turned what would have been negative news into an opportunity to make the move and found an apartment of his own.*

Sometimes we anticipate the possibility of a negative in our lives and prepare a Plan B, just in case. At other times, we find it appropriate to design a Plan B on the spot to soften the jolt of an incoming negative. Either way, we can be successful in keeping a negative from being a permanent fixture in our perceptual field.

Technique 3:
Use a hypothetical "converter" to turn negatives into positives.

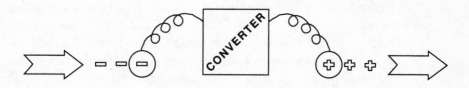

Sometimes a jolt can be used to our advantage. For example, assume that you have been thinking about a permanent relationship with a person, and she or he unexpectedly decides to close out the affair. How might you use your "make-believe" converter? You immediately focus on all the problems you might have been stepping into and compensate by deciding you need to spend more time on your career anyway so you will be in a better position to assume a permanent relationship later. In short, *you use the jolt to make yourself into a better person.* Here is another example:

> *Victoria has been highly motivated at work. For the last year, she hoped to be appointed to the role of manager. Yesterday, she discovered she had lost out to someone from another department who she felt was less-qualified. Did Victoria become negative and "sulk"? Not on your life! Rather, she kept her positive attitude at work. But she also quickly brought her resume up to date, arranged for some interviews, and two months later was hired as a vice president in a competitive firm.*

Victoria used her ability, track record and attitude to convert what could have been a long-term negative into a positive.

Major Negatives Require a Different Treatment

During a lifetime, everyone is on the receiving end of some major or highly traumatic blows. This is part of life. These events often hit so hard that it takes months or years to overcome their effects. It can seem like a person's perceptual field has turned totally negative and then, to top it off, someone steps on it.

Regaining your focus and confidence is a major undertaking. Such "blows" normally fall into one of three categories:

Relationship Losses—Mutually rewarding family, personal and professional relationships constitute the very fabric of living. When such a relationship is lost, it can be a severe blow. The death of a close family member, a divorce or a "conflict" separation are examples. Blows in this category can run deep and require a long fight back.

> *Three years ago, Jerry received custody of his 15-year-old daughter. Immediately, his life changed. It was shopping with Lisa, going to school events, and making a major effort to be both father and mother. An entire, wonderful lifestyle was built around her. Then, she decided to build a career in the military and was gone. It took Jerry a full year to make even a partial adjustment.*

Health Problems—Thanks to the advances of modern medicine, more and more people are surviving accidents, heart attacks and/or diseases that, in the past, often spelled death. The climb back is not a physical recovery alone. It also entails a major attitude adjustment. The mental challenge of regaining a positive focus can continue long after the physical problems have been corrected.

> *Miranda lost track of the number of visits she made to her plastic surgeon after her accident. During the following two years, she tried to stay out of sight of everyone, except a few close friends and family members. She was afraid to return to the mainstream and resume her career until her "restored image" was in place. Once she became adjusted to her new, still attractive face, Miranda accepted the challenge of building a new focus on life. Her plastic surgeon could go only so far.*

Career Set-Backs—The loss of a job, being passed over for promotion, or making the wrong career move at the wrong time can temporarily take a person down for the count. Often it takes months before the individual is ready to climb back into the career ring and become productive again.

Cy was proud of the fact that he had made three career moves since graduating from his university, five years ago. Each move meant more responsibility, more opportunity and more financial rewards. Then, perhaps because he became overconfident, he accepted a job in New York City that only lasted four months. Cy soon discovered that the recession was real. His skills were not in demand. His attitude became negative. It took him over six months after he had hit bottom to get a good start climbing a new corporate ladder.

The Attitude Recovery Pyramid

Naturally, most of the minor jolt techniques can be used as part of a more comprehensive and time-consuming program, designed to help one adjust to *major blows*. Here is a recovery approach you may wish to tuck away for future use:

The illustration below presents a bird's eye view of the recovery steps that are often recommended by experts as necessary to get back on top of things after a major setback.

ATTITUDE PYRAMID

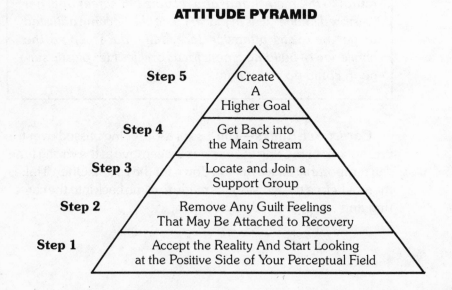

Step 5 — Create A Higher Goal

Step 4 — Get Back into the Main Stream

Step 3 — Locate and Join a Support Group

Step 2 — Remove Any Guilt Feelings That May Be Attached to Recovery

Step 1 — Accept the Reality And Start Looking at the Positive Side of Your Perceptual Field

Step 1:

According to clinical professionals, you cannot start your climb back to the top unless you first recognize that the event really happened and there is nothing you can do to change things. If love is gone, you cannot bring the same relationship back. If a close relative or dear friend has died, he or she can continue to inspire, but not participate. If a job has been eliminated, it is necessary to find another. The best way to make your first move back is to start looking at what remains, not what has been lost.

> *It took Jeremy over a year to realize his wife Cindy was out of his life forever and Kitty, their only child, would be a weekend daughter. Only when he fully accepted this reality, was he able to start to rebuild a life of his own.*

Step 2:

A feeling of guilt over something that has taken place in the past can become an ongoing negative in one's perceptual field. It drags attitude down and performs no useful purpose. It is bad enough to "cry over spilled milk." It is much worse to *remember* the mistake, accusing yourself over and over again, for months and years ahead. Until guilty feelings are completely removed, upward progress is slow, if not impossible.

> *Looking back, Jeremy realized that he had not been a good communicator. As a result, Cindy had not felt the same degree of personal growth that he was enjoying during their six years of marriage. She often felt left out and it was mostly his fault. When he accepted his mistake and the guilt that went with it, he realized that Cindy was probably going through the same process herself. He decided it made no sense to victimize himself any longer.*

Step 3:
Almost every community has a support group to help those who have suffered a major trauma. These groups often meet informally on a regular basis. The champion of all support groups is Alcoholics Anonymous.

> *When Jeremy was invited by a close friend to join a "Parents Without Partners" group, he was less than enthusiastic. But, feeling the need to gain greater understanding, he decided to attend a session. After three meetings, he discovered his problem was not much different from that of others. He was not alone. He learned how to make his weekends with Kitty more rewarding. His attitude improved. Soon he put his "Parents Without Partners" group at the top of his list of "no miss" activities.*

Step 4:
Eventually, the dark clouds that are created by a major blow must be dissipated through activities centered around fresh goals. Many people stop smoking while recovering from the loss of a loved one and dedicate the success they achieve to that person. Others accept the loss of their jobs by starting a skills improvement program and enrolling in a local college. Some lose themselves in work and enjoy recognition through their increased on-the-job efforts. All such positive activities assist individuals in getting back into the mainstream of living.

> *Everyone knew that Jeremy was well on his way to building a new life for himself when he got involved in an exercise program, bought a new car, and started dating. It was also obvious in his on-the-job productivity, which increased as his positive focus on life improved.*

Step 5:

Just getting back into the mainstream after a major blow is usually not enough to sustain the progress of most people. After rebuilding themselves, they frequently feel they should set higher goals for themselves. And they do!

> *It took almost three years, but when Jeremy had adjusted to his new life as a bachelor he wanted to demonstrate to himself, and especially to Kitty, that he was on a new, more successful career track. He wanted to communicate, without words, that he had accomplished personal growth, had established some new goals, and was optimistic about the future.*

ATTITUDE PYRAMID

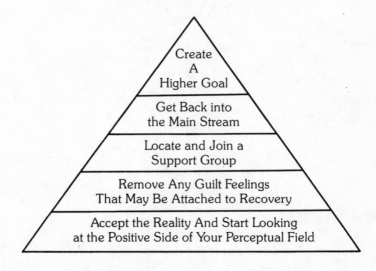

Create
A
Higher Goal

Get Back into
the Main Stream

Locate and Join a
Support Group

Remove Any Guilt Feelings
That May Be Attached to Recovery

Accept the Reality And Start Looking
at the Positive Side of Your Perceptual Field

Each individual must find and climb her or his personal trail back to the top of the attitude pyramid. Many can make the journey without professional help. Others wisely seek and find a counselor, psychologist or psychiatrist to help them find a direction that will allow them to achieve new heights. Those who achieve success following a major blow often discover a new maturity within themselves and a new appreciation of their attitude. Having fought their way back into the mainstream, their perception is more insightful than ever.

Chapter 11

You've Got To Be Headed Somewhere

You've Got To Be Headed Somewhere

> *"Destiny is not a matter of chance, it is a matter of choice; it is not a thing to be waited for, it is a thing to be achieved."*
> **William Jennings Bryan**

Goal-oriented people tend to be more positive than others. The primary reason for this is because they are so involved in reaching their goals that they do not have time to dwell on negatives. It is a credible formula. Once they reach one challenge, they create another. They never stop.

When you have a goal that you earnestly wish to reach, the goal becomes a positive factor in your mental focus. In other words, *a goal established today becomes a plus factor you did not have in your perceptual field yesterday.* If it is a realistic, reachable goal, you are motivated to reach your potential. The goal will shine brilliantly in your mind, like a bright star in a constellation. Because of it, other positive factors in your perceptual field will sparkle more clearly.

GOALS ARE POSITIVE FACTORS

If goals can do so much to improve attitudes, why then, do so many people drift aimlessly? These individuals refuse to accept the premise that a strong, realistic, motivating goal automatically pushes negative factors to the outer perimeter of their thinking. *They reject the idea that a new or revised goal — one that will provide a new focus — may be the greatest gift they can give themselves.* Best of all, it is free!

Goals Are Positive Factors

Everyone was discouraged by Martin's apparent inability to do anything meaningful with his life. He moved from one unimportant job to another. When he accumulated a little money, he would disappear and surface later. Then, he fell deeply in love with Jodi. It quickly became apparent that Jodi, a high-school counselor, was goal-oriented. If their relationship was to last, Martin would have to be headed in some direction. With her understanding and influence, Martin discovered he wanted to be a teacher. He returned to college for a graduate year and a credential. A marriage and three children later, Martin still gives Jodi credit for giving his life meaning and direction. "Most of all, she has inspired me to stay positive during difficult times. We talk openly about our attitudes and the impact they have on our careers and children. We think we are more positive as a team than we would be alone, mainly because we have both personal and family goals."

In the pages ahead, you will be introduced to four goal-producing opportunities. Please explore each possibility carefully because you will be asked to indicate your preferences at the end of the chapter. This approach will help you in two ways:

1. You will be able to assess your present goals to see if they are adequate as far as keeping a positive attitude is concerned. If you feel your present goals are "doing the job," you will be reinforced to continue to reach your goals with more enthusiasm. Knowing you are on the right track is always helpful.

2. You may discover that it is time to give yourself some new goals that will contribute significantly to your attitude. This could be the most important discovery you can make.

Please take one possibility at a time and be ready to make your selection on pages 124 and 125.

Opportunity #1:
Select a New or Improved Leisure Goal

Many people spend so much time and effort "working" that they understandably neglect leisure activities.

> *Steve works hard at his job and tries to keep positive factors ahead of the negatives. When he gets home, Steve digs in on home problems to back up his wife, who also works outside the home. When the day finally ends, there is barely enough time to enjoy a television show, let alone plan an event for the weekend. Steve is so tired planning the other aspects of his existence that he makes little use of his leisure time. Result? He is negative most of the time.*
>
> *On the other hand, Clark and his wife give leisure planning top priority. They never start a week without having agreed upon a weekend goal that they both anticipate with enthusiasm. Their normal procedure is to talk things over Sunday and not make a decision until both are in agreement. Whether a ski trip, going to the theater, giving or*

attending a party, or simply going out to dinner, they plan ahead. Both agree that having a goal gives their week extra meaning and they accomplish more.

The failure to set leisure goals—for daily, weekends, and vacation periods—is a major mistake, because a single goal can illuminate and expand the positive side of one's perceptual field.

INJECT AN EXCITING LEISURE GOAL INTO YOUR PERCEPTUAL FIELD

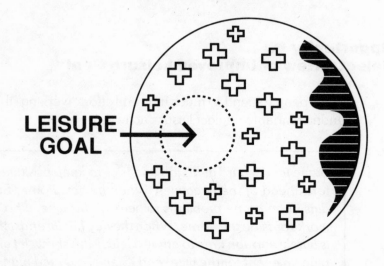

LEISURE GOAL

Most people need specific leisure goals to remain motivated to take a lighter view of their jobs and devise ways to shorten the time devoted to home tasks. All work and *no planned leisure* gives Jack a negative attitude. If there is not enough time during the week, the only solution is a weekend devoted primarily to some fun and fulfillment.

Everyone needs a leisure goal to insert into the positive side of their perceptual field. Most activities fall within the following categories:

Sports	Selective T.V./Video
Travel	Nature
Hobbies	Special events
Indoor games	Reading

Add your own: _____

_____

_____

_____

_____

No one can specify a motivating leisure goal activity for another. We all have desires that may not appeal to others. The problem is recognizing and giving them priority. For married couples, it usually means a degree of compromise and/or granting enough "space" for the other to do their own thing. Most important of all, the leisure activity selected must be converted into a goal. It must be a desire strong enough to lift one above work and home tasks.

> *Darlene is a single parent who has a demanding telemarketing job. She spends most of her workday on the telephone, dealing with prospects and clients. Each day, a few tend to be abusive. On the way home from work, Darlene must pick up her 4-year-old daughter, fix dinner, complete household tasks and also deal with her own problems. What saves Darlene? Two things: some quality time each night with her daughter, plus a planned leisure activity each weekend — either a day trip or a social involvement. The activity is always planned ahead of time and takes priority over everything else.*

> *Anthony is a route delivery person who must keep to a tight schedule and produce at a high level. His boss is demanding. The truck he drives is ten years old, and his routes often involve fighting heavy traffic. When Anthony arrives home, he is worn down physically. By the time he helps with chores, he is lucky if he can stay awake for a single television program. What saves Anthony? He loves golf and with blessings of his wife, he plays 18 holes each Saturday as part of a lively foursome. During the week, Anthony dreams and talks golf. On Saturday he plays. Next to his wife and family, golf is the biggest positive in his life.*

Opportunity #2:
Insert a New High Risk Goal into
Your Perceptual Field

As previously mentioned, we all have a number of positive factors upon which to focus. What we often fail to realize is that we can create and inject new "positives" anytime we desire. In short, *we can create our own perceptual fields.*

> *Mr. Leslie was vice president of a major corporation on the Pacific Coast for over ten years. When his operation was moved to Chicago, Mr. Leslie and his family made the move, too. But, neither he nor his family adjusted well to the new environment. Result? Mr. Leslie set a new goal for himself. He would start a business of his own back in the same coastal community he left. From the moment he made his decision to return to his desired life style, his perceptual field became more positive and his new attitude was primarily responsible for the success of his enterprise.*
>
> *Marge and her sister Sylvia were inseparable as they grew up. After college, Marge set out on an exciting career path and moved to another state. Sylvia married a hometown*

sweetheart and had a daughter. When Sylvia and her hus-band were killed in a private airplane crash, Marge strug-gled with the idea of adopting Sylvia's child, but was concerned over whether she could maintain a growing career and raise the child, too. Finally, she decided to give herself a double goal. The additional goal of being a par-ent gave her life new meaning. And, with the love the child brought into both of their lives, there was an immediate upgrading in the way she looked at life.

Sometimes circumstances arise that lead individuals into creating new goals for themselves. New goals can also be created by research and pure determination. For certain people, creat-ing a significant new goal may be the best way to improve the positive side of their perceptual fields.

Can you create a new goal and insert it into the positive side of your perceptul field?

Opportunity #3:
Convert an Existing Positive Factor
Into a Major Goal

You probably already have a plus factor in your perceptual field that can be made into a goal. For example, you might recognize that your family is a major positive element, yet you still may take it for granted. Then, perhaps a new child arrives, or your relationship is threatened and you suddenly realize: "Hey, I need to do more to make this family a better place for all of us." When thoughts such as this one are converted into specific goals such as spending more time at home or remodeling a room or taking more family vacations, then the conversion is working.

CONVERTING A POSITIVE INTO A GOAL

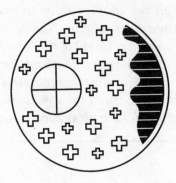

When goals are specific, less mind-time is devoted to negative thinking, and efforts to reach the goals reverse the normal negative drift.

> *For three years, Frank had been piling up negative factors in his life — health problems, financial reverses, divorce. You name it, Frank experienced it. During this difficult period, he found release and therapy through bicycling. It was his number one plus factor. To get a fresh start on life, Frank established a personal goal to devote more time to cycling. He bought a new bike, joined a cycling club and met new friends. By expanding one of his few remaining plus factors, Frank achieved a goal that made a major improvement in his attitude. This, in turn, helped him survive a tough period in his life.*
>
> *A series of negative events during the year caused Fran to comment: "This is the one year in my life I would like to forget." After the year ended, Fran, always a staunch temple member, decided to make a stronger commitment to her religion. Within a few weeks, she was appointed chairperson of a new member visitation committee. Soon, Fran was so involved in positive activities that, without*

knowing it, she had pushed the negative factors in her life into the background. Everyone noticed the difference in her attitude.

With three children to care for, a large home to maintain and a devoted husband who nevertheless required much attention, Estelle had all the goals she needed to stay upbeat. Even so, once the children were in school, she found herself turning negative. Answer? She became involved in a "Save The Forest" project and within a few weeks made an attitude turnaround. Before her involvement in her new project, nature had been a major plus factor in her perceptual field. A nature walk had always done wonders for her attitude. By expanding her involvement, she made the positive side of her perceptual field more positive.

Everyone has positive factors in their perceptual field that can be developed and expanded. The best way to accomplish this is by giving these factors more time and more signficance.

Do you have a positive you would like to convert into a goal? If so, write it in the space below.

_____

_____

_____

_____

_____

_____

_____

CONVERTING JOB FACTORS INTO GOALS

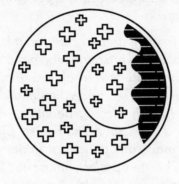

For over a year, William has felt buried among many other young employees at his large technical firm. Last month, to make himself stand out in the crowd, he decided to communicate a more assertive image. The moment he made this commitment, he started to feel better. With a specific goal, he could feel some of his negative attitudes dissipating. The result? William improved his wardrobe, contributed more at all staff meetings and submitted in writing an idea for better productivity that had been on his mind for some time.

Tammy could not figure it out. When she listed the positive factors about her job, she realized it would be difficult to duplicate her position elsewhere. Yet, she knew her productivity was slipping, along with her attitude. How could she remedy the situation? She decided that the best way for her to gain recognition would be to increase her skills through self-improvement courses that would increase her productivity above that of other co-workers; at the same time, she would work to become more popular among her co-workers. In her efforts to reach both goals, Tammy became so busy that she did not have time for her previous negative attitudes. Even her boyfriend noticed the difference.

Do you have a work-oriented "positive" that you can convert into a major goal? If so, write it in the space below:

_____

_____

_____

_____

_____

Opportunity #4:
Transfer a Negative into a Positive and Then Convert It into a Special Goal

It is an accomplishment to turn an existing positive into a goal. However, you will achieve more if you are able to first convert a negative into a positive *and then convert it into a goal.* This means you take a negative from one side of your perceptual field and transplant it to the other side. Then you make a goal out of it. Tricky maneuver? Perhaps, but you will get an idea of how it works from the following examples:

FROM A NEGATIVE TO A POSITIVE INTO A GOAL

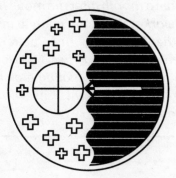

Anne

> *Anne has had a weight problem for eight years. Her blood pressure has climbed and her attitude has fallen. She has made many attempts to solve the problem and improve her image. Usually they were very ambitious but soon failed. Nothing worked. A few months ago Anne joined a weight control program with two friends. This time she established a reachable weight loss goal for herself and stayed with it. Result? Not only has she lost the weight she set as an initial goal, her life is measurably brighter, because she converted a negative factor into a positive one. Instead of being depressed, she is proud of her achievement and has committed herself to continue.*

Robert

> *For four years, Robert worked full-time and was also a care provider for his aging mother. Despite the fact that he carried his burden with grace, the added burden was a downer in Robert's life. Encouraged by a close friend, he finally made the difficult decision to place his mother in a care facility. Within a month after the move had been made, everyone at work noticed the change in Robert. Now he visits his mother frequently. Even better, the visits are positive experiences for both parties. Most importantly, now Robert has his own life. Eliminating a giant negative factor and replacing it with pleasant visits — no guilt, has given Robert a new outlook.*

Hector

> *When Hector turned 55, his attitude started going down-hill. A supervisor in a furniture factory, he thought all that might be ahead for him was an early death or a dull retire-ment. Then, his company offered those over 55 a chance to attend a retirement seminar. As a result, Hector started to view retirement as a second chance at life. In effect, he traded a negative in his life for a positive. Instead of being discouraged by the future, the seminar convinced him to enjoy the life he had earned. The result was that Hector decided to take early retirement and even joined a health club a few months before he retired.*

A weight problem, having to care for an elderly parent, and reaching middle age can all be negatives that one might convert into positive goals.

Here are two job-oriented situations:

Conner

> *Conner was so upset emotionally over a long-standing conflict with his boss that his productivity had dipped to an unacceptable level. His attitude was lower than his productivity. Conner decided he would confront his superior over the conflict. If it did not lighten things up, he would resign. Fortunately, the conference started some honest communication, and the result was a resto-ration of the relationship. Eventually, his superior became his number one supporter. Instead of a negative that was pulling Conner down, the relationship became a posi-tive that gave Conner a new lease on his job and life.*

Sara

> *Sara, a talented, hard-working employee, knew she was contributing much more to the success of the department than any of her co-workers. One day Sally said to Sara: "What are you knocking your brains out for? Where is it taking you?" When Sara started thinking about it, she became depressed over her situation. But instead of letting it get to her, she decided to work even harder. Result? Two things happened. The department was reorganized—Sally was transferred to a less-desirable job and the supervisory job was given to Sara. Persistence on her part had turned what might have been a negative into a positive.*

Most people have existing negative factors that can be turned into positive challenges. A good idea is to take some reflective time every so often to review your perceptual field to see if a "turnaround" opportunity exists. Those who are able accomplish turning negatives into positives are the big winners in their careers and lives. History is filled with examples of great people who have converted a negative into an opportunity.

Selecting Your Best Opportunity

Which gift—opportunity—are you going to wrap up and present to yourself? What challenge fits into your comfort zone? What action will contribute most toward changing your life for the better? Four choices are listed below. Place a check mark (✔) opposite the one that is best for you.

I plan to:

☐ Give myself some new or revised leisure goals that will provide enjoyment and fulfillment over a long period of time. This may mean my scrapping a current goal. My new goals may be expensive, or require research or lengthy discussions with my friend or spouse. It may even mean simplifying my home tasks to generate more time to devote to the goal. Whatever it takes, this may be my best opportunity to balance my life and improve my attitude.

☐ Create a new goal that has not been a positive factor in my perceptual field. To accomplish this, I plan to make a list of possibilities and carry it around with me until I become enthusiastic about an item. I will consider things such as learning to play a musical instrument, learning to fly an airplane, receiving a higher academic degree, etc. I will seriously consider anything that has crossed my mind that would give me a sense of achievement. Once I have a list of possibilities, I pledge to study and analyze my options. Then I will narrow the list down through discussion with others. In making a final choice, I plan to follow my inner desires. Once the decision is made, I will mentally insert my new goal into the positive side of my perceptual field. *Then I will go for it!*

☐ Select a positive factor that already plays a role in my perceptual field and make a more significant goal out of it. I promise to consider such possibilities as devoting more time to traveling, turning a hobby into a business, or building an exciting new career. If my job is dull, I will work to turn something I am already good at into a major campaign. Once I make my choice, I will set up a strategy to reach it. To some people, keeping a major goal a secret is more motivating that sharing it with others. It is my goal, my choice! My life!

☐ Take a close look at the negative factors in my perceptual field and choose one that has conversion potential. This means selecting a negative I can redesign and transfer to the positive side, where I can make it into an important goal. This, of course, is a difficult decision. I expect to use caution in making my choice, but will not back away from one that will make a major difference in my life. Once a goal-decision has been made, I will start the transfer process by establishing a number of smaller goals that will help me reach my major goal. Once I have reached my first target, I know that I will have taken my first step toward a new, more constructive attitude. I will have discovered that life is better when I am headed somewhere!

Chapter 12

Questions From The Back Row

Questions From The Back Row

> *"What a wonderful life I've had. Only wish I had realized it sooner."*
>
> *Collette*

Please imagine that you are participating in a seminar where the topic is attitude, and your leader is willing to answer questions about attitude.*

Can one person help another have a more positive attitude?

This is a common question. Usually the individual asking has a son, daughter, spouse or close friend in mind.

The best answer is to suggest to the person wanting help that he or she say nothing, but strive instead to be a good model. Attitude is difficult to talk about directly. This is especially true of a person with whom you have a close relationship. The best way is to be positive and hope the individual will either pick up on the spirit or allow an opportunity to openly discuss attitude in a sensitive way, without it becoming a threat to the other person's self-esteeem.

One helpful thing to keep in mind is that when we become impatient with the negative attitudes of others, we need to remind ourselves that being a good model will pay dividends. Staying positive for *yourself* is the most important thing you can do.

---

* All questions have been asked of the author on numerous occasions.

What can I do when I start my day in a negative mood?

Try to refocus on positive factors in your perceptual field as soon as possible. To do this, it may be necessary to quickly enter an activity that will cheer you up. For example, you might talk to a friend who is usually positive, or tell a funny story to a co-worker. Maybe it is something as simple as a second cup of coffee. You might even start singing or whistling. For some, it might mean wearing something dramatic, in their favorite color.

Once you have performed the activity that is positive, you can then direct your mind to one good aspect of your life—for example, your health or the success you are having in a certain area. Positive thoughts will help you lock in your positive attitude for the day.

Many people use preventive techniques before they start each day. One man keeps a picture of his favorite vacation getaway on his wall at work, so he can constantly think about the beauty of the scene during each day. Others may start the day reading an inspiring message from a book, or perhaps singing loudly in the shower. A growing number use exercise as a great way to kick off each day.

To each his own, just so it works.

What other suggestions might assist people in staying positive?

This is a big order! We all have secret ways to hold on to our positive attitudes.

One technique might be to give part of your positive attitude away. When we share our positive attitude by doing helpful things for others who are negative, we are in fact, helping to sustain our own positive attitude.

There also is a connection between our self image and how positive or negative we are at any given time. Staying in good physical shape through exercise, plus good grooming, new hair styles, etc. help us look good to ourselves.

On top of everything, we need to keep a sense of humor.

People who use a concept known as the "flipside technique" have an advantage. This means facing a problem by turning it over to see if there is any humor that will make it less damaging.

We all need to learn to use every trick and strategy available. Of course, these tricks should fit into our comfort zone. This means the technique is something we can do naturally. One older woman has a "crazy hat" she keeps in a closet when she is positive, and wears immediately when she knows she is becoming negative. Other people have similar tricks that work for them.

Why is a good image so important to attitude?

Consider a 15-year-old girl who is pretty but has yet to build a good image of herself. She tries to hide school pictures and refuses to talk about her appearance. Somehow, her perception of herself is not what it could or should be. She looks better to others than she does to herself.

This same situation is serious with people of any age, because if a person does not perceive him or herself in a good light, that individual will lose confidence and this will subsequently cast a shadow over the way he or she interpret her life.

The 15-year-old girl needs encouragement from her family and teachers about her appearance. She needs friends. A role in a school play or some other form of recognition would help. It is not a matter to be taken lightly. If a correction is not eventually made, a person's basic attitude toward life may be skewed toward the negative, because that individual does not have a positive self-image.

Can we be victimized by those we love who have negative attitudes?

Yes. We can become victims when our friends or relations become permanently negative factors in our perceptual fields, and we are unable to create an offsetting counterforce. For example, if our spouse turns negative and destroys our marriage, it is easy for us to become a victim. Or, perhaps one of our elderly parents becomes critical and negative. In turn, this can change us into becoming a victim. The list of examples is endless. Such situations often will dominate the negative side of our ability to focus and often will push positive factors into the background.

How can we keep from being victimized by those that mean the most to us?

A positive attitude is so priceless that we should never allow another person, even those we love most, to turn us negative on a permanent basis. There are two reasons for this: First, if we turn negative, we lose our advantage in helping the other individual. Second, we are not being fair to ourselves. Our attitude belongs only to us. If we permit another individual to turn us negative, we are giving them permission to own a very special part of us. This is the part that gives us beauty, joy and fulfillment. When someone important turns us negative, we must use every technique to keep our perceptual field positive. With some personal relationships, this may require us to take drastic measures we have avoided in the past. Here is an example:

It was a second marriage for both Brent and Francine. They were extremely happy for three years; then Francine became negative, primarily because of worries connected with Penny, her daughter from her first marriage. In an effort to save their marriage, Brent said he would welcome Penny to live with them for one year, until she was able to square herself away. He would give her a job in the business he owned. If, however, the experiment did not work, Penny must leave and Francine must adjust to the situation without losing her positive attitude. She must protect her own attitude, no matter what happens to Penny. Fortunately, Penny put her life together in less than six months, used the skills she had learned to get another job, and moved out with a more positive attitude herself. With one risky gesture, Brent not only saved his marriage, but he also helped improve the attitudes of two others.

Sometimes it is necessary to create temporary negative factors to rid ourselves of negative factors that could turn out to be permanent.

How are attitude and expectancy related?

When an individual keeps looking on the positive side of life, something magical can happen. Positive factors tend to grow into a state of expectancy that normally cause other good things to happen. For example, professional salespeople say the best time to make a difficult sales call is immediately after a sale has been made to another party. If two or more sales are made in succession, the salesperson is "on a roll."

There appears to be a direct correlation between what people expect and what really happens. When a baseball player falls into a hitting slump, it can continue because the player becomes negative and does not expect to get a hit. How might this be reversed? Somehow, the player needs to form a picture of getting a hit. Perhaps imaging might help. Or maybe he or she just needs to relax, enjoy some laughter and forget about the slump. This may allow regaining concentration and getting a hit.

What about attitude and leadership?

Few people will follow a negative leader for long. Followers want to be led to a positive goal that will make life better. Sure, they expect their leaders to deal with tough problems and make good decisions, but they want them to remain positive during the process.

What is the relationship between learning and attitude?

There is a measurable correlation between how much a person learns and that individual's attitude toward the subject to be learned. When faced with a difficult learning assignment, one path toward success is to seek out and concentrate on the positive aspects of the subject matter. If a student has a boring and ineffective teacher in a required course, one solution is to look for the positive aspects of completing the course, regardless of how boring the instructor happens to be. To accomplish this might require a tutor or some independent reading, but with the right attitude, success is possible.

Overachievers—those students who do better than their test scores indicate—usually have a positive interest toward learning. They may learn some things more slowly, and it may take more effort, but, to compensate, they are often better at applying what they have learned. As long as they do not stress themselves into emotional problems, they are successful.

Underachievers—those who function below their ability indicated by test scores—often tend to permit a few negative factors to sidetrack them. Because of their negative attitudes, they sometimes become unfairly critical of teachers. They allow themselves to get bored when it is not necessary. In short, their attitudes often cause them to learn less than overachievers.

If you learn to replace a negative mind-set toward learning with something more positive, you are on the road to achieving virtually any goal you desire. For example, if you realize a personal computer with a word processor would improve your performance, but have an attitude that keeps telling you that you cannot learn to operate a computer, you tend to make all kinds of excuses. In short, you resist making full use of a terrific tool, simply because your negative attitude prevents you from learning.

What is the relationship between attitude and a sense of humor?

A person with a positive attitude, by definition, also possesses a sense of humor. The two simply go together. Those with a sense of humor save the ability to interpret what they perceive in a light-hearted manner. They have a mind-set that causes them to look for the light side. A negative person rarely looks for humor.

The relationship between humor and attitude is symbiotic. One enhances the other. When a storyteller gets laughter, it stokes that person's attitude. Even when laughter is forced by the listener, they come out ahead. Attitude and humor are partners. It is a mutually rewarding relationship.

***How can people who must live with major negatives in
their lives cope?***

Obviously, not all negative factors in one's life can be reduced
in size or pushed into the background. Some tend to stay center
stage most of the time. But the more such factors can be kept
in the background, and there is an adequate supply of positive
factors upon which to concentrate, the more positive an
individual will be.

The trick, of course, is to *accept reality but not let it turn you
negative.* An excellent example is Jim Abbott, a pitcher for the
Los Angeles Angels. He was born with a stub for a right hand.
Not only has he developed into an outstanding pitcher, but he
can also make difficult fielding plays along with the best of them.
Somewhere along the line, Jim Abbott accepted the reality of
his situation, but decided that with the right attitude he could
not only make it to the major leagues, but become a star per-
former. A person's ability is only limited by his or her attitude.

What is the difference between a mood and an attitude?

A mood is an emotional disposition. Attitude is a mental
process. Although emotionally based, moods can often be traced
to attitudes. For example, if you show up for work in a happy
mood, but a variety of negative factors pop up during the day,
you might leave work depressed or angry. Concentrating on
negative work related matters has the ability to turn your mood
sour. On the other hand, you could show up for work in a bad
mood and, because the workday is made up of positive factors,
your mind—attitude—can lift you out of your bad mood. What
this means is that those who are able to maintain an upbeat attitude have less trouble with mood swings, both on and off the job.

***Why is so much emphasis placed on the visualization
of perceptual fields?***

This is an excellent question. The reason for using graphics
to illustrate perceptual fields is to encourage readers to *form men-*

tal images of the way they look at life from the inside. This process—called imaging by psychologists—has many advantages. Following are three reasons for keeping a visualization of a perceptual field in your mind:

1. Keeping a model perceptual field quickly helps you realize when your attitude is out of focus, and you need some form of adjustment.

2. Imaging has certain psychological advantages as far as telling you what kind of corrective action to take. In other words, through visualization, you can see opportunities to make adjustments that otherwise would be overlooked.

3. Some people foolishly avoid daydreaming and fantasizing. Those who understand how creating positive illusions can neutralize negatives and can improve a focus on life, are fortunate. How many times have you heard a special person talk about his or her "dream"?

Do people who concentrate excessively on positive factors develop Pollyanna attitudes and lose their ability to solve reality problems?

There is little indication that people who consistently maintain a positive focus in life avoid reality. In fact, it may be the other way around. Mature, positive individuals that engage in positive illusions, often face responsibilities and problems better than those who are more negative.

For example, when a problem surfaces, positive people want to solve it quickly, because they do not want it to grow or continue nagging them. Negative people, on the other hand, tend to avoid taking action and ultimately pay the price of procrastination. Most business leaders agree that a positive approach to a problem usually brings a better and faster solution.

***Do people who do the best at staying positive back away from
reality and ignore nasty problems that need to be solved?***

Some positive people do run away from responsibilities. But
most positive people seem to do a better job of handling responsibilities and making tough decisions than their negative colleagues. This happens for two reasons. First, positive people tend
to tackle tough problems to protect their focus on life. Second,
it often takes a positive attitude to face a tough problem in the
first place.

For example, a business executive may pride herself on her
positive approach. However, when she faces a difficult problem,
she attacks it head on, even if it means temporarily turning negative. Once a decision has been made, she can quickly return to
a positive focus. It would appear that such a person uses a positive attitude to reach a better decision, even though outwardly
she seems negative during the process. This person is able to
accept the negative consequences of reality on a temporary basis
and then quickly restores her focus on the more positive factors
within her perceptual field. It might take some understanding
by staff members and employees, but this kind of leader should
be respected.

Then, there is the aspect of maintaining good mental health
so that one can face the realities of everyday life over the long
haul. A positive viewpoint will keep us in a better position to deal
with reality "bumps" as they occur.

People who assume great responsibilities must possess a positive attitude. Perhaps that is the underlying reason they are
leaders in the first place.

***Is it reasonable to claim that maintaining a positive
focus constitutes an immune system against poor
mental health?***

To a great extent, yes. There is some debate about the
therapeutic value of a positive attitude and its component, laughter. It is reasonable to claim that together they can constitute a

psychological immune system that will protect you from frequent "down periods." For example, now and then the reality of living can send us into a "blue funk," which can seem like a bottomless hole. Fortunately, most holes have a ladder. No matter how far we fall, we can concentrate on the positive side of our perceptual field and—one rung at a time—climb out of our down period. Usually we climb out by ourselves. Sometimes the "hole" is deep enough that it requires the help of friends and perhaps a professional.

Is there a correlation between the amount of money one has accumulated and a positive attitude?

It would seem that individuals who have more money or have higher than average incomes would have more positive attitudes than those who are not so fortunate. This is not always the case. Money alone does not produce a positive attitude. There are many negative people who have a fortune. Sometimes, they worry so much about what to do with their money, it turns out to be a negative factor.

Earning money is a goal—and as previously stated, goal-oriented people are usually more positive, because they have less time to worry about the negatives in their lives. There is no reason to believe that the goal of earning money is less effective in producing positive attitudes than other goals.

It would be easy to fall into the trap and say that money puts one in a position to *buy* a positive attitude. Money allows one to buy possessions, but having more possessions does not translate into having a positive attitude. Attitude is perceptual and many people, regardless of income or wealth, perceive a more simple, beautiful world around them than those with many possessions. All of this is simply to say there is little, if any, correlation between wealth and a positive focus on life. Those in lower income brackets should not use it as an excuse to be negative. Those in higher income brackets do not have a license on being positive.

Does a positive attitude bring happiness?

It sure helps! But simply having a positive attitude offers no guarantees.

As parents, we can give our children many things. We can, for example, help them build healthy bodies through good nutrition, exercise and rest. We can also give them education so they are better prepared for the realities of life. Sometimes, it is even possible to give a child some power. And, of course, a parent can provide money and possessions. What parents cannot provide is a guarantee of happiness.

Why is this?

Happiness is very personal. It is a feeling of joy that may be available to an individual when everything is just right *for that person*. This means that each individual must put his or her own formula for happiness together, without expecting help from others.

It is a most elusive blend of many factors that produces happiness. No one can predict ahead of time just what this blend may be or how long it will last. It would appear, however, that a positive attitude is at the top of the list. Put another way, a person with a positive perspective will open the door more widely to the possibility that happiness will enter and stay longer.

It seems that the younger generation is more concerned with attitude than their parents. Is there any evidence this may be true?

There is no evidence to support this possibility. Some people claim "older" generations may be more negative because of stresses caused by war, economic recessions, the sexual revolution and so forth. These same individuals often say that the current new generation, those from 20 to 35, appear to have more insight relative to the importance of attitude in their lives.

They seem intrigued by the concept and use the word more in their communications.

One final question. What would you want to remember about attitude five years from now?

If nothing more, at least that you, the reader will accept the perceptual aspects of the attitude concept and realize that you control what you see in your world. When you are able to perceive the beauty surrounding you—talk about it—feel it—taste it—hear it—then you should thank your positive attitude for making your life more worth living.

One final wish is that you learn to pass on your special interpretation of attitude to those who are important in your life.

Good things should be shared.

Chapter 13

Life Is Today!

Life Is Today!

> *"Many people's tombstones should read: Died at 30. Buried at 60."*
>
> **Nicholas Murray Butler**

You frequently hear the expression, "I take it one day at a time." This communicates, in essence, that life today is more complex than I care to handle all at once. But give it to me one day at a time, and I can cope. Comfortable little philosophy!

A slight variation on this theme is for someone to say: "I *live* one day at a time." It may appear to be splitting hairs, but this version is more positive. To "take" one day at a time sounds defensive, like a person is standing up to barrage of negatives. To *live* one day at a time communicates that some quality time is envisioned during the next 24 hours.

Consider, for example, a person who contracts AIDS through a blood transfusion. Things are not fair and are tough. But a cousin of mine who has this problem usually winds up our telephone conversation by saying: "My wife and I are living one day at a time and making the most of it." The phrase "making the most of it" represents a true "attitude believer." With the right attitude, it is possible to have a beautiful day under almost any circumstance.

Two actual cases represent the "one day at a time" attitude. One man, age 70, has been retired for 13 years. He is highly negative, without any apparent reason. He seldom leaves home. A neighbor man, older than him, often frequents amusement parks to ride roller coasters and other thrill rides. When the older man was asked how he was able to maintain such a zest for life, he answered: "At this stage of life, time is short, and I want to live one day at a time!"

If you accept the philosophy that biting off small chunks of life is smart because they are easier to deal with, you are in good company. In a way, a single day can be a microcosm of a full life. If you could isolate one day from a complete life for analysis, what would constitute a happy day? How should it start? How might it end? How would you design it?

LIVING ONE DAY AT A TIME

Lifetime   **One Year**   **One Month**   **One Day**

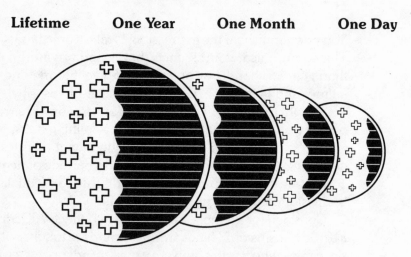

The Positives and Negatives of a Single Day

On the positive side, you might have such factors as a tennis match, a theater party, seeing a special person, achieving an important work goal and so on—joys of the day! On the negative side, you might have such factors as a dental appointment, getting your car repaired, cleaning up the house and so on—life's little negatives!

There are countless techniques you can use to convert a negative into a positive day. See example on page 161.

FROM NEGATIVE TO POSITIVE IN A SINGLE DAY

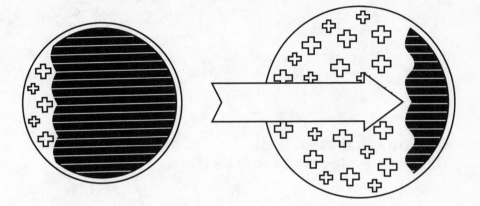

You might:

- Treat yourself to a special purchase.
- Share a funny story.
- Have lunch at a new, exotic place.
- Do something special for a neglected friend.
- Wear something new or offbeat from your wardrobe.
- ADD YOUR OWN:

_____

_____

There are other advantages to the take-a-day-at-a-time approach. Here are a few:

- You can start each day with a clean slate. This is not so easy with a complete life.
- It is easier to deal with a single day because the factors do not have long-range significance. No BIG decisions need to be made.
- Major problems can usually be postponed without "spoiling" the day upon which you are concentrating.

- Having a couple of good days in succession can do wonders as far as creating a new, longer-range perspective. When you are down, you have got to crawl before you walk, walk before you run, etc.

- After a major setback, creating a positive day can rebuild your confidence. It can give you a "bridge" that will restore the positive perspective you previously had on life.

One Day at a Time is a Recommended Recovery Pattern

When should you try to forget the big problems of life and settle for one day of fulfillment? When should you trade your total perspective for a miniature?

The answer is when you need a new perspective. When your normal perceptual field is clouded, when you are down in the dumps, and when you have lost confidence. During these periods it makes good sense to start on a small scale. It is especially effective when coming back from a traumatic experience, such as a relationship breakup or major surgery.

When the medication started to wear off, Milt realized he was in an intensive care unit. He did not know if a full recovery was possible. Even if it was, he knew it would be weeks or months away. Milt knew a strict routine would be mandated in the hospital and a day-by-day pattern would need to be maintained when he got home. The prospect appeared bleak. How could he deal with it? Milt decided he had to push the long-range future aside and live life hour by hour. He quickly discovered that little events became big events. Breakfast was the equivalent of a night on the town. Television became a gala opening on Broadway. A telephone call became a special event. As his progress accelerated, Milt decided that living one day at a time, and not expecting too much, had advantages. He made a vow to appreciate the little things in life when his recovery was complete.

Jon lost his job six months ago. He has yet to receive a new job offer. At the beginning, Jon accepted his situation as a challenge. He read books on how to get a job, listened to experts and formulated a master plan that would lead him to a better opportunity. Nothing happened. Now Jon is down to one day at a time. He tries to make appointments on one day and go through interviews the next. This approach has helped him to relax, find better interviews, and present himself better. Yesterday, Jon received his first solid job offer.

Lori was discouraged after receiving an average rating on her last formal appraisal. In talking it over with her boss, Lori was told that all it would take to make a major improvement would be for her to increase her concentration. "Stop worrying about the big things beyond your control and concentrate on the little things that will increase your productivity. Take it one day at a time." Fearful of losing her job, Lori took the suggestion seriously and discovered, within a week, that she was more positive on the job and her productivity was higher.

Returning to a Daily Focus to Fight Negative Drift

Attitude maintenance takes time and energy, even when things are going smoothly. What about times when negative drift starts to take over? When fate seems to be dealing you problems instead of pleasures? Are these the times you should refocus on one day at a time?

Genevieve seems to turn sour on life three or four times a year. Really sour! She has no idea what causes the down periods, but she knows when they arrive. Her solution? She

> *immediately shifts gears and starts living one day at a time. She literally discards all of her big, life-sized problems and accepts the fact that she is in the clutches of negative drift. Then, slowly, day by day, she starts her climb back to her normal, positive existence. How does she do this? By living with little, simple, positive perceptual fields that can last only a day. Then, two or three days later, she is ready to tackle the reality of a bigger world.*

Having a Specially Designed Daily Lifestyle

Observation and interviews confirm that we all have our own daily patterns of living. As an author, I have either a "writing day" or an "activity day." Each has a separate pattern. Most people have working day patterns and weekend or holiday patterns. Listed below are a few tips that you might wish to incorporate into your own patterns:

- Many people start each day with a set of positives that gets their day rolling in an upbeat manner. On workdays, Edgar does a short workout, enjoys a shower, has his first and only cup of real coffee with a simple breakfast, reads the comics, and heads for his job.

- Fran makes a point of having a positive, interesting conversation with one special person before mid-morning. An office manager, Fran gets to work early and selects from her large staff one person with whom she can exchange positive small talk for a few minutes.

- Work satisfaction of some kind is usually necessary for most people. Jim, an advertising account executive, tries to come up with a fresh idea every day. When he fails, he retrieves an old idea, takes a fresh approach, and gives it a new twist.

- The idea of doing one special thing each day to make life better for others has appeal. Grace maintains a large circle of friends and a support system by doing little things for those who are working through tough situations. Some days it is nothing but a telephone call. Grace claims this is the way to make *her* days.

- Early evening goals help to make up the patterns many people follow on work days. Max reserves a full hour each evening to play with his three children—or do what they request. It is quality time that contributes to the way he views life.

- Late-in-the-day goals constitute a reward most people claim provides the attitude boost they need to get through the day with style. With Maria, it is nothing more than time to read a chapter in a good novel before turning the day over to sleep.

Daily Living Patterns Plus Long-Term Goals May Provide The Perfect Formula

In this chapter we have said that living one day at a time is an excellent way to recover from a major blow. We have also suggested that having a daily lifestyle pattern is an excellent way to "maintain" a positive attitude when things are normal. Is there something missing? Something that needs to be added? Normally, yes. There is a third element that needs to be introduced, which will support and augment the "recovery" and "maintenance" aspects of attitude. The missing ingredient is having a long-term goal.

Knowing you are heading somewhere with a predetermined purpose can provide the motivating "power" to live one day at a time in the first place. Such a goal can also encourage you to design and live a daily and weekend pattern that will enhance your attitude. Here is a case that incorporates all three of the elements.

For the last two years, Toni has been positive 95 percent of the time. This is far more so than earlier in her life. It started when she had a double mastectomy. Instead of giving up, she slowly adopted the live "one day at a time" philosophy. It was not easy, but once back on her career track as an architect, she perfected it by giving each workday a special "design" and each weekend a special "pattern." Toni did so well with her recovery that she became a volunteer counselor to help other women recover from the same operation. This helped; however, she discovered that there remained an "emptiness" in her life, and she fought to avoid falling into a negative malaise.

Then, one summer she had a rewarding experience vacationing at a small ranch. Toni discovered that the experience took her back to her childhood, as a child of a rancher. For the second time in her life she fell in love with horses. The clear, cold ranch evenings gave her life a spiritual meaning that had been missing. The following summer she returned to the same ranch for her vacation.

One evening, Toni learned that the ranch was going to be put up for sale the following year. One thing led to another, and Toni decided she wanted to make owning the ranch her retirement goal. She would work another five years. In the interim, her recently divorced daughter would operate the ranch.

Once the goal had been formulated and financial arrangements completed, Toni discovered that she had found the missing element in her personal formula for happiness — having a long range goal. This goal provided Toni with the motivation to make even more of her day-by-day philosophy. She expressed it this way: "Everyone needs a significant goal to make life more exciting. I have noticed too many people drag themselves through life. Not me! Every day is going to be complete for me. Just wait and see!"

Expectancy is the key. No matter how a day starts out, with an attitude of positive expectancy something good will turn up. The same is true in the bigger picture. The more you expect out of the various phases of life—childhood, adolescence, adulthood, retirement—the happier you will be. Many threads need to be woven into the fabric of a life—love, adventure, work, achievement, luck—but the brightest, strongest and most important thread is attitude.

Attitude makes it happen!

Chapter 14

Let Your Attitude Give You A Better Life

Let Your Attitude Give You A Better Life

> *"God gave us memory that we might have roses in Deceember."*
> **James M. Barrie**

Whether or not your realize it, as you moved from chapter to chapter in this book, you were given TEN mental strategies to maximize the positives and diffuse the negatives in your life. The more you use these ten planning skills, the more positive your life will become. Life enhancement is, in effect, a matter of attitude.

PERCEPTUAL STRATEGIES

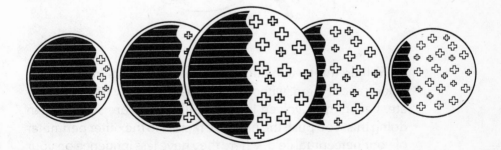

In this chapter, in reviewing the ten strategies, you may wish to rate each one as far as your personal comfort zone is concerned. A scale, from 1 to 10, is provided at the end of each summary. If you give yourself a rating of 8, 9 or 10, you are saying that it works for you currently use it—or you intend to apply it immediately. If your rating is somewhere in the middle, from 4 to 7, you are saying that the strategy could help you become more positive but, at this point, it is not top priority. If your rating is 3 or under, you are receiving a signal that the approach is not within your comfort zone and you should eliminate it as a possibility.

Strategy 1:
Concentrate Or Focus Your Mind On The Positive Factors That Currently Exist In Your Life

You do this by thinking about positive factors (mind-time), talking about them (without over-doing it) and, when appropriate, becoming involved in them. When you are successful in doing this, you push the negative factors to the outer perimeter of your perceptual field, where they have less influence on your attitude.

Rollie has more negatives in his life than most people. This is because he has a withered leg caused by polio when he was a child. His physical activities have always been restricted. This helped Rollie discover that concentrating on negatives is a lost cause. As a result, he has trained his mind to focus on positives. Result? Rollie is a very skillful computer programmer, successful in business, a joy to be around, and highly respected. Ask him why he has accomplished so much and he replies: "It's attitude. I look for the positive features in people, my job, my environment, and my wife and children. Life is too short to dwell on negatives."

Please rate yourself.

CONCENTRATING ON THE POSITIVES

1	2	3	4	5	6	7	8	9	10

Strategy 2:
Change The Way You Look At Work

Generally speaking, when an individual is consistently negative at work, three choices are available:

1. Find a similar job with another organization.

2. Retrain yourself for a new, different career.

3. Change the way you look at your present job.

Switching to a new job is possible, but is not always easy or wise. Preparing for a new career is usually a time-consuming, expensive and demanding undertaking. A recommended approach is to seriously consider the third option before selecting one of the first two. The most practical approach is often the best.

What about you? Are you as enthusiastic about your job as you would like to be? Have you been underestimating your present job and career? Is growth possible? Are you a fun person to work with? Is your job worth keeping if it makes you negative?

Two factors need to be considered. First, it is easy and natural to blame management for your situation. Such a course leads nowhere. And second, few people can be negative at work and positive away from work. One environment tends to impact the other, so negative workers often pay a double price.

If you admit your focus on work could improve, why not look inside yourself and assume that tomorrow you are going to work in your present job for the *first time?* This empowers you to have control over your attitude and means you have the capacity to view your present job in a more positive way.

HOW I VIEW MY JOB TODAY

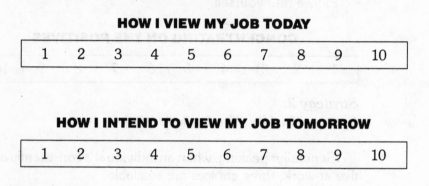

| 1 | 2 | 3 | 4 | 5 | 6 | 7 | 8 | 9 | 10 |

HOW I INTEND TO VIEW MY JOB TOMORROW

| 1 | 2 | 3 | 4 | 5 | 6 | 7 | 8 | 9 | 10 |

Strategy 3:
Create Positive Illusions And Sprinkle Them On The Positive Side Of Your Perceptual Field

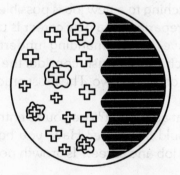

You create a positive illusion when you imagine or dream about something that may be beyond reality. You paint yourself into a scene where you play a key role, even though it exists only in your mind. Everyone does a little of this, and as long as these illusions are not carried too far, they have a tendency to supplement "real" positives in your perceptual field. Some people believe that by adding illusions (the cloud symbols in the graphic) you can actually improve your mental health.

Frank is a regular jogger. His pace is modest and he would never be a threat to win a race. This does not prevent Frank from dreaming about winning a major race during one of his frequent "fun runs." By thinking about his potential to win an event, he has actually improved his times so that he often will establish a "personal best" even though he still finishes in the middle of the pack.

Mindy has had an over-sized imagination since she was a small girl. This has changed her life in two major ways. First, she has become a movie buff, because they often deal in fantasies. Second, she has become a professional librarian, because she is in a better position to pick and choose what she wants to feed her mind. When asked why she seems so happy, Mindy replies: "I think it is because I have found a good balance between my dreams and reality. By selecting the right books and movies, I fill my mind with positives instead of negatives that seem to burden most people I know."

How do you feel about creating illusions? Please rate yourself.

CREATING ILLUSIONS

1	2	3	4	5	6	7	8	9	10

Strategy 4:
Invest More In "Happy Talk"

With so much media attention devoted to negative events, it often seems increasingly difficult to maintain positive, enjoyable and humorous conversations with others. Yet, excessive negative talk can focus so much attention on negative factors that one's perspective is altered.

How do you keep this from happening?

The answer is to discipline your talking. Listen to yourself. If you discover you are reinforcing the complaining conversations of others, or introducing negatives into your conversations (i.e., have I told you about my aching back?), switch to upbeat topics. A little "happy talk" is necessary if you are to protect your positive attitude.

This does not mean you cannot take stands or positions on controversial subjects, or fight for a cause dear to your heart. It simply means that finding fault, discussing how others annoy you, and forcing others to hear about your ailments is a good way to victimize yourself. Without knowing it, your life can increasingly turn negative and you will have mainly yourself to blame.

HAPPY TALK SCALE

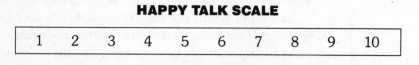

| 1 | 2 | 3 | 4 | 5 | 6 | 7 | 8 | 9 | 10 |

Strategy 5:
Discover A New Goal

You need not be satisfied only with the current positive factors in your life. You can also come up with a new, fresh, dynamic goal that will give your life new meaning. This can start anytime, including today! Sometimes a goal as simple as dedicating yourself to making another person happy through a visit or phone call can do the trick. As long as your goal is in harmony with your personal values, it does not matter what the goal itself may be.

Manuel grew up in a fatherless family in a Hispanic ghetto. The negatives in his life were often associated with a lack of money. Manuel decided at an early age that he could be more positive and help his family if he found a way to attend college so he would qualify for a high paying position. Today, Manuel is a vice president of a large utility. When asked how he maintains his highly positive attitude, he states: "The best thing that ever happened to me was being born poor and understanding that with hard work things had the potential to get better. Everything is a matter of attitude, but I really owe much of my success to a wonderful high school teacher who encouraged me to set a goal of going to college. I've been setting goals for myself ever since. My current goal is to help my two children prepare themselves academically for college."

ESTABLISHING NEW GOALS

1	2	3	4	5	6	7	8	9	10

Strategy 6:
Learn To Make Decisions Quickly

It is almost impossible to be a consistently positive person, while at the same time carry a growing list of unsolved problems.

Procrastinating may give the outward impression that all is well, but deep inside procrastinators know they are turning negative. Why? Because accumulating problems tends to increase and enlarge negative factors within a person's perceptual field.

Those who face up to problems and work to quickly solve them have learned how to keep negatives *out of their minds*. Those who drag around with an overload of problems and postpone finding solutions consume mind-time with negative factors. This, in turn, usually leaves them more negative.

Most people who treasure their positive attitudes develop procedures to help them solve problems quickly and correctly. They face the situation, get the facts, weigh them and then, sometimes after consulting with others, take action. This does not mean they always avoid mistakes. Mistakes are made. It does mean, however, that they probably make fewer mistakes because they follow a procedure and enter the problem-solving process with a positive focus. Also, they learn from their mistakes and do not repeat them. They know that action is better than procrastination.

You cannot hold on to old problems and fight off new ones without it "getting to" your attitude. It is better to suffer the consequences of a poor decision than to refuse to take action until your focus is cluttered with unsolved problems that are using up your mind-time.

DECISION-MAKING SCALE

1	2	3	4	5	6	7	8	9	10

Strategy 7:
Eliminate Relationships That Drag You Down

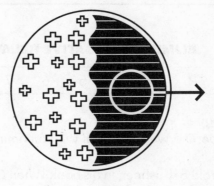

Having meaningful relationships with others is a great way to add positives in your life. No person is an island. We all need the love and support of others to keep our attitudes in high gear. But just as relationships can do a great job building us up, a few can also tear us down. When you become involved in a negative relationship and you have devoted sufficient time to improve it without results, it may be time to end or distance the relationship to protect your happiness.

> *Mary Jean did everything she could think of to get along with her stepsister Raylene. Mary Jean's father had married Raylene's mother before Raylene left home, and the tensions that developed between the two caused Mary Jean to leave home before she was ready. Even so, she made every effort to resolve the conflict. The family gatherings where she made her attempts were most difficult. In talking the situation over with her boyfriend one evening, he told Mary Jean, "Look, you've done everything in the book that you know to build a better relationship. It just doesn't seem to work. It's time you back away and protect yourself. When it comes to people, you can't win 'em all. If you*

> *don't stay clear and wash her out of your mind, you'll do nothing but hurt yourself. Maybe in time, staying away will improve things. In the meantime, I'll help you all I can."*

ELIMINATE NEGATIVE RELATIONSHIPS

1	2	3	4	5	6	7	8	9	10

Strategy 8:
Improve The Way You Deal With Incoming Negatives

Harold S. Kushner, in his book *When Bad Things Happen To Good People,** makes the point that no one is immune to bad things happening. Blaming others, including God, only turns us more negative. Instead, we should protect loving relationships with others, so we can call on them for help when it is needed.

It also helps to have certain techniques and strategies "in place," so we can adjust when bad things happen. Sometimes minor downers can be disposed of before the day is over. At other times, incoming problems can be converted into opportunities. Major blows require both time *and* help from others. In addition, certain behaviors will bring better results. *These behaviors can be learned.*

Just as people act ahead of time to protect their material possessions (fire insurance, safety deposit boxes, alarm systems, etc.), it is possible to establish ways to protect your most priceless possession of all—your positive attitude!

Attitude "believers" understand how difficult it can be to cope with incoming negatives. They also have developed techniques to help them fight off negatives that are encountered on a day-to-day basis. Thus, they design daily patterns to keep themselves positive. When a major blow hits, they use all of their tricks—and never hesitate to go to a professional for help.

---

* Schocken Books, 200 Madison Avenue, New York, 1989

How do you rate the system you are currently using to protect your positive attitude?

ATTITUDE PROTECTION SCALE

1	2	3	4	5	6	7	8	9	10

Strategy 9:
Convert Positive Factors In Your Perceptual Field Into Goals

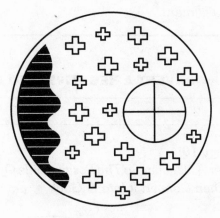

Often we take certain positives in our lives for granted. For example, we may neglect family members that we love or we may enjoy membership in an organization without contributing as much as we should. And we often forget to share certain experiences with friends who can help us stay positive.

As an only child, when Heather's father died she inherited his mountain home where she had enjoyed happy times. Having retired the previous year, she decided to keep the home for herself and spend as much time as possible in the mountains. One fall evening, after she had gathered wood and built a warm, inviting fire, Heather felt lonely. She decided a second marriage was out of the question and it was too late to adopt a child. Yet she realized that she probably had 20 or 30 years ahead of her. Then it came to her! Talking to herself she said, "My church has always been a real positive in my life. Why not give my life meaning by donating this home to the church as a mountain retreat for members, as well as myself?" The following week Heather presented the idea to her minister and the trustees. They were delighted and, from that moment on, the feeling of loneliness was gone. Heather had converted a positive in her life to a major goal that was to bring her involvement, new friends, and a sense of fulfillment.

CONVERT A NEGATIVE INTO A POSITIVE

1	2	3	4	5	6	7	8	9	10

Strategy 10:
Transfer A Negative To The Positive Side Of Your Perceptual Field And Then Convert It Into A Goal

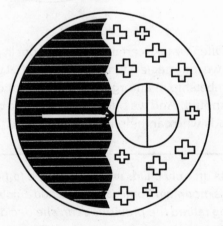

Often people tend to avoid this plan because it sounds too difficult. They will not take the time to understand how it might work for them. This is a natural reaction. Yet, the benefits can be so rewarding that the idea deserves analysis. For example, you might have a negative, destructive relationship with an individual—child, boss, spouse—and then, through counseling and a change in attitude, it is possible to have a reconciliation. Great! Then, with work, you go one step further and turn what has been improved in the restored relationship into a major goal.

Because of feelings Francis never understood, he grew up with a hostile attitude toward his father. After his mother died, the resentment increased. Then, one evening, while watching a movie with a similar father-son relationship, he suddenly started crying. He realized he had been unfair to his father for years and that the whole thing had been a burden that had hurt his attitude toward life.

Francis, knowing how much his father enjoyed fishing, decided to act. He invited his dad on a one-week fishing excursion in Mexico. His father accepted and they had a great opportunity to communicate and get to know each other. As a result, Francis was able to move the relationship with his father from the negative to the positive side of his mind. Then, he took a final step and committed himself to keeping the relationship alive and healthy. In discussing the matter, Francis said, "I spent forty years in needless conflict with my father. Now I intend to make up for it. You can't believe how much better life is with my new attitude."

CONVERT A NEGATIVE INTO A POSITIVE AND THEN INTO A GOAL

| 1 | 2 | 3 | 4 | 5 | 6 | 7 | 8 | 9 | 10 |

It would probably be a mistake to try to implement more than one or two of the strategies at once. Why not select the one you rated the highest to start with, and later incorporate others which may be within your comfort zone? Keep in mind that only you can deal with your own attitude.

Chapter 15

Call On Your Attitude For A Better Life

Call On Your Attitude For A Better Life

> *"Things turn out best for people who make the best of the way things turn out."*
>
> *Art Linkletter*

At last! Whether you recognize it or not, reading this book has revealed the wonders of your attitude. You have been shown that your attitude is priceless. It dominates all of your other personality characteristics. Only you can understand and appreciate your true attitude.

You have read examples of how attitude goes up and down on a daily basis and learned that attitudes mirror experiences of the world outside. Best of all, you have discovered that you alone control your attitude which, in turn helps control your life.

Attitude is Something Like a Miracle Camera

It is one thing to know that your attitude helps you to view the world in the way you wish. It is something else to look inward and try to figure out the psychological process that determines how this miracle occurs. A superficial way to do this is to build an image of your attitude as a mentally controlled, fully-automated, high-tech, super-responsive "camera" that you can point in whichever direction you wish. This miracle "camera" functions during all of your waking hours. It also operates on a strange, fragmented basis when you dream. When you focus in the direction of positive, happy factors, you feel good. When you focus on negatives—well, you know the answer.

It is not a good idea for most of us to devote too much time worrying about how our attitudes work. We should leave that to folks like clinical psychologists. Instead, we should take it on faith that others like people with positive attitudes.

Lighter Ways to View Your Attitude

Let us assume that you love music. When you hear your special kind of music, you brighten. Music helps you adjust your focus away from negatives, toward positives. Why not think of your attitude as a kind of "transmitter" that can convert the vibes you send it—your kind of music—into a more positive way of looking at things?

Or assume that you find yourself falling into negative periods too often. You seem to continually worry about how things are going. You feel you are on the receiving end of too many problems. In these situations, smart people call on their attitude for help. Believe it or not, your attitude is always receptive to your request to improve a situation. When you learn you are able to call in your attitude and say: "Please help me laugh more at life. Give me the power to look at the funny side of things so I can dissipate my problems through laughter. If I can laugh more, it will help me be more positive."

What if you find yourself being frequently hurt by others? What if you try to develop meaningful relationships, but it does not seem like you receive the attention you give out? What can you do if relationships do not live up to your expectations?

Why not view your attitude as an ally that has the capacity to turn people-misunderstandings into positive relationships? For example, ask your attitude this question: "How can I learn to see the good in people?" The answer might be something like this: "Looking for the good in people, regardless of their background, is a matter of attitude. When you *want* to see good things, they will appear."

Working Closely With Your Attitude is The Answer to a Better Life

All of this "speaking to your attitude" business may seem foolish, even childish. But it is a way to maintain control. People talk to their cars, tools, pets and houseplants to make them perform better. Why not coax better performance from our attitudes through self-talk? Most successful people, in one way or another, give ongoing "pep talks" to their attitudes.

Here are a few examples of how people get in touch with their attitudes.

Carl was 32 years of age before he consciously spoke to his attitude. Two events precipitated the contact. First, he had a surprise break-up with his girlfriend. Second, he broke his jaw in a construction accident and suffered through having it wired almost shut for two months. When Carl became aware he was spending too much time "feeling sorry" for himself, he switched from talking about himself to others, his former practice, and went directly to his attitude. It worked.

Once his recovery was complete, Carl told a close friend, "The first thing I had to do was to recognize I was negative, but that otherwise, I was okay. Then, I had to tell my attitude over and over that I was in control. Finally, I accepted support and encouragement from friends like you. The support was there all the time, but my negative attitude wouldn't let me accept it.

Nobody ever told me that my attitude was the center of my life. Nobody ever suggested that I sit down and talk to my attitude, and that if I could change the way I look at things, I could turn my life around and get back on the beam. I can tell you this. I have really turned out to be a believer."

Richard and Fanny were approaching fifty and everything was in focus. Their three children were out of the nest and a new sense of freedom surrounded them. They had just purchased new gear for their future camping trips. Then, without warning, things got complicated. Richard was given the "golden handshake" by the company where he had worked for nearly twenty-five years. Fanny was faced with holding down her office job and being a care provider for her mother who lived nearby. Richard had to go on unemployment insurance, with no job replacement in sight. During the same period, he started having dental problems.

One Friday night, when Fanny arrived home, Richard had their camping gear packed and was ready to roll. They took off for a favorite campsite in the mountains. That night, after Fanny was asleep, Richard sat under a tree and started talking about his problems with himself. All Richard's voice said back as he turned in for the night was: "It may sound like you are having tough luck, but your real problem is attitude." As he absorbed the beauty surrounding him, he thought, "Richard, you fool, you came from a positive family, you have a great wife who is helping with family problems and you are doing nothing but making it harder for her. You have always been a positive guy. Maybe that's your problem. You've taken your positive attitude for granted and you can't do that. You are becoming a victim to yourself. Look at all the beauty around you! It is not the world itself that has gotten you down, it is your failure to look for the positive things." Suddenly, Richard knew he was in control again. He could feel that his attitude would be better starting tomorrow. He felt so good he wanted to whistle, but held back because it was 2:00 A.M. and Fanny was sleeping.

When Maggie's husband died, she knew she had lost more than a lover, companion and provider. She had also lost the support she needed to stay positive. Tom was the attitude believer in the family. He made a habit of looking on the bright side and teasing others into doing the same. Tom was always telling funny stories, always making others feel better about themselves. When Maggie would have down periods, Tom would buy her crazy things to cheer her up. When she did not respond, he would lay it on the line. "Look here, Maggie," he would say. "You need to get in touch with your attitude and get back on the ball. All you are doing is pampering yourself."

It has been seven years since Tom died, but Maggie claims that Tom still shows up at the bottom of her bed some nights and talks to her. "Honestly," she claims, "when I get down on myself, he seems to appear and says things like 'Maggie, you've got to look at what you've got, not what you have lost. Go do something foolish tomorrow and get your attitude back so I can be proud of you.' And would you believe it, I wake up in the morning ready to take a new shot at things."

Get in Touch With Your Attitude

We all need to get in touch with our attitudes now and then. We must each do it in our own way, in the right setting, and alone. If you hear the expression, "get in touch with yourself," it really means the same thing, because your attitude is, in effect, yourself.

What is an Attitude Believer?

Attitude believers are people who have discovered they can control their focus on life *and that it makes a difference*. Believers are those who regularly pull themselves out of down periods with help from their attitudes. They have handled tough problems and come through smiling. Believers *know* the power of a positive attitude. They understand that working closely with their attitudes is the best way to cope.

Unfortunately, most people do not become attitude believers early in life. It is only after their positive attitudes have successfully pulled them through some difficult situations that they enthusiastically jump on the band wagon.

Just reading this book, or parts of it, will not, by itself, make you a believer. Some of the ideas, techniques or strategies that fit into your personal comfort zone, however, will help. You need to test them. When you find something that works, you will become a believer, and you will have learned a secret about how to win at the game of life.

The sooner you believe, the better your life will become.